What is Anthropology?

Anthropology, Culture and Society

Series Editors:
Professor Thomas Hylland Eriksen, University of Oslo
Dr Jon P. Mitchell, University of Sussex

What is Anthropology?

Thomas Hylland Eriksen

Pluto Press
LONDON • ANN ARBOR, MI

First published 2004 by Pluto Press
345 Archway Road, London N6 5AA
and 839 Greene Street,
Ann Arbor MI 48106, USA

www.plutobooks.com

British Library Cataloguing in Publication Data
A catalogue record for this book is available from the British Library

ISBN 0 7453 2320 0 hardback
ISBN 0 7453 2319 7 paperback

Library of Congress Cataloging in Publication Data applied for

—

10 9 8 7 6 5 4 3 2 1

Designed and produced for Pluto Press by
Chase Publishing Services, Fortescue, Sidmouth, EX10 9QG, England
Typeset from disk by Stanford DTP Services, Northampton, England
Printed and bound in the European Union by
Antony Rowe Ltd, Chippenham and Eastbourne, England

'Make everything as simple as possible.
But not simpler.' (Einstein)

'He who speaks no foreign language
knows nothing about his own.' (Goethe)

Contents

Part 1
Entrances

1
Why Anthropology?

A generation ago, anthropology was scarcely known outside of academic circles. It was a tiny university subject taught in a few dozen countries, seen by outsiders as esoteric and by insiders as a kind of sacred knowledge guarded by a community of devoted initiates. Anthropologists went about their fieldwork in remote areas and returned with fascinating, but often arcane analyses of kinship, slash and burn horticulture or warfare among 'the others'. With a few spectacular exceptions, the interest in anthropology from the outside world was modest, and its influence was usually limited to academic circles. Only very rarely did it play a part in the public life of the anthropologist's own society.

This has changed. Growing numbers of non-academics in the West have discovered that anthropology represents certain fundamental insights concerning the human condition, applicable in many everyday situations at home. Its concepts are being borrowed by other university disciplines and applied to new phenomena, its ideas about the need to see human life from below and from the inside have influenced popular journalism, and student numbers have grown steadily, in some places dramatically. For example, at the University of Oslo, the number of anthropology students grew from about 70 in 1982 to more than 600 a decade later.

In many western societies, anthropology and ideas derived from the subject became part of the vocabulary of journalists and policymakers in the 1990s. This is no coincidence. In fact, it can be argued that anthropology is indispensable for understanding the present world, and there is no need to have a strong passion for African kinship or Polynesian gift exchange to appreciate its significance.

There are several reasons why anthropological knowledge can help in making sense of the contemporary world. First, contact between culturally different groups has increased enormously in our time. Long-distance travel has become common, safe and relatively inexpensive. In the nineteenth century, only a small

3

proportion of the western populations travelled to other countries (emigrants excluded), and as late as the 1950s, even fairly affluent westerners rarely went on holiday abroad. As is well known, this has changed dramatically in recent decades. The flows of people who move temporarily between countries have grown and have led to intensified contact: business-people, aid workers and tourists travel from more economically developed countries to less economically developed ones, and labour migrants, refugees and students move in the opposite direction. Many more westerners visit 'exotic' places today than a generation ago. In the 1950s, people may have been able to go on a trip to Rome or London once in their lifetime. In the 1980s, people could travel by Interrail to Portugal and Greece, and take similar trips every summer. Young people with similar backgrounds today might go on holiday to the Far East, Latin America and India. The scope of tourism has also been widened and now includes tailor-made trips and a broad range of special interest forms including 'adventure tourism' and 'cultural tourism', where one can go on guided tours to South African townships, Brazilian *favelas* or Indonesian villages. The fact that 'cultural tourism' has become an important source of income for many communities in the less economically developed world can be seen as an indication of an increased interest in other cultures from the West. It can be a short step from cultural tourism to anthropological studies proper.

At the same time as 'we' visit 'them' in growing numbers and under new circumstances, the opposite movement also takes place, though not for the same reasons. It is because of the great differences in standards of living and life opportunities between more and less economically developed countries that millions of people from non-western countries have settled in Europe and North America. A generation ago, it might have been necessary for an inhabitant in a western city to travel to the Indian subcontinent in order to savour the fragrances and sounds of subcontinental cuisine and music. Today there are large numbers of Indian restaurants in many western cities, ranging from four-star establishments to inexpensive takeaway holes in the wall. Pieces and fragments of the world's cultural variation can now be found on the doorstep of westerners. As a result, the curiosity about others has been stimulated, and it has also become necessary for political reasons to understand what cultural variation entails. Current controversies over multicultural issues, such as religious minority rights, the *hijab* (shawl or headscarf), language instruction in schools and calls for affirmative action because of ethnic discrimination in the labour market testify to an urgent need to deal sensibly with cultural differences.

Second, the world is shrinking in other ways too. Satellite television, cellphone networks and the Internet have created conditions for truly global, instantaneous and friction-free communications. Distance is no longer a decisive hindrance for close contact; new, deterritorialised social networks or even 'virtual communities' develop, and at the same time, individuals have a larger palette of information to choose from. Moreover, the economy is also becoming increasingly globally integrated. Transnational companies have grown dramatically in numbers, size and economic importance over the last decades. The capitalist mode of production and monetary economies in general, globally dominant throughout the twentieth century, have become nearly universal. In politics as well, global issues increasingly dominate the agenda. Issues of war and peace, the environment and poverty are all of such a scope, and involve so many transnational linkages, that they cannot be handled satisfactorily by single states alone. AIDS and international terrorism are also transnational problems which can only be understood and addressed through international cooperation. This ever tighter interweaving of formerly relatively separate sociocultural environments can lead to a growing recognition of the fact that we are all in the same boat; that humanity, divided as it is by class, culture, geography and opportunities, is fundamentally one.

Third, culture changes rapidly in our day and age, which is felt nearly everywhere in the world. In the West, typical ways of life are being transformed. The stable nuclear family is no longer the only common and socially acceptable way of life. Youth culture and trends in fashion and music change so fast that older people have difficulties following their twists and turns; food habits are being transformed, leading to greater diversity within many countries, and so on. These and other changes make it necessary to ask questions such as: 'Who are we really?', 'What is our culture, and is it at all meaningful to speak of a "we" that "has" a "culture"?' 'What do we have in common with the people who used to live here 50 years ago, and what do we have in common with people who live in an entirely different place today?' 'Is it still defensible to speak as if we primarily belong to nations, or are other forms of group belonging more important?'

Fourth, recent decades have seen the rise of an unprecedented interest in cultural identity, which is increasingly seen as an asset. Many feel that their local uniqueness is threatened by globalisation, indirect colonialism and other forms of influence from the outside, and react by attempting to strengthen or at least preserve what they see as their unique culture. In many cases, minority organisations demand cultural rights on behalf of their constituency; in other cases, the state tries to slow down or prevent processes of change or outside influence through legislation.

Our era, the period after the fall of the Berlin wall and the disappearance of Soviet-style communism, the time of the Internet and satellite TV, the time of global capitalism, ethnic cleansing and multi-ethnic modernities, has been labelled, among other things, the age of globalisation and the information age. In order to understand this seemingly chaotic, confusing and complex historical period, there is a need for a perspective on humanity which does not take preconceived assumptions about human societies for granted, which is sensitive to both similarities and differences, and which simultaneously approaches the human world from a global and a local angle. The only academic subject which fulfils these conditions is anthropology, which studies humans in societies under the most varying circumstances imaginable, yet searches for patterns and similarities, but is fundamentally critical of quick solutions and simple answers to complex questions.

Although the concepts and ideas of anthropology have become widely circulated in recent years, anthropology as such remains little known. It is still widely believed that the aim of anthropology consists in 'discovering' new peoples, in remote locations such as the Amazon or Borneo. Many assume that anthropologists are drawn magnetically towards the most exotic customs and rituals imaginable, eschewing the commonplace for the spectacular. There are those who believe that anthropologists spend most of their lives travelling the world, with or without khaki suits, intermittently penning dry, learned travelogues. All these notions about anthropology are wrong, although they – like many myths of their kind – contain a kernel of truth.

THE UNIQUENESS OF ANTHROPOLOGY

Antropology is an intellectually challenging, theoretically ambitious subject which tries to achieve an understanding of culture, society and humanity through detailed studies of local life, supplemented by comparison. Many are attracted to it for personal reasons; they may have grown up in a culturally foreign environment, or they are simply fascinated by faraway places, or they are engaged in minority rights issues – immigrants, indigenous groups or other minorities, as the case might be – or they might even have fallen in love with a Mexican village or an African man. But as a profession and as a science, anthropology has grander ambitions than offering keys to individual self-understanding, or bringing travel stories or political tracts to the people. At the deepest level, anthropology raises philosophical questions which it tries to respond to by exploring human lives under different conditions. At a slightly less lofty level, it may be said that the task of anthropology is to create astonishment, to show that the world is both richer and more complex than it is usually assumed to be.

To simplify somewhat, one may say that anthropology primarily offers two kinds of insight. First, the discipline produces knowledge about the actual cultural variation in the world; studies may deal with, say, the role of caste and wealth in Indian village life, technology among highland people in New Guinea, religion in southern Africa, food habits in northern Norway, the political importance of kinship in the Middle East, or notions about gender in the Amazon basin. Although most anthropologists are specialists on one or two regions, it is necessary to be knowledgeable about global cultural variation in order to be able to say anything interesting about one's region, topic or people.

Second, anthropology offers methods and theoretical perspectives enabling the practitioner to explore, compare and understand these varied expressions of the human condition. In other words, the subject offers both things to think *about* and things to think *with*.

But anthropology is not just a toolbox; it is also a craft which teaches the novice how to obtain a certain kind of knowledge and what this knowledge might say something about. Just as a carpenter can specialise in either furniture or buildings, and one journalist may cover fluctuations in the stockmarket while another deals with royal scandals, the craft of anthropology can be used for many different things. Like carpenters or journalists, all anthropologists share a set of professional skills.

Some newcomers to the subject are flabbergasted at its theoretical character, and some see it as deeply ironic that a subject which claims to make sense of the life-worlds of ordinary people can be so difficult to read. Many anthropological texts are beautifully written, but it is also true that many of them are tough and convoluted. Anthropology insists on being analytical and theoretical, and as a consequence, it can often feel both inaccessible and even alienating. Since its contents are so important and – arguably – fascinating, this only indicates that there is a great need for good popularisations of anthropology.

Anthropology is not alone in studying society and culture academically. Sociology describes and accounts for social life, especially in modern societies, in great breadth and depth. Political science deals with politics at all levels, from the municipal to the global. Psychology studies the mental life of humans by means of scientific and interpretive methods, and human geography looks at economic and social processes in a transnational perspective. Finally, there is the recent subject, controversial but popular among students and the public, of cultural studies, which can be described as an amalgamation of cultural sociology, history of ideas, literary studies and anthropology. (Evil tongues describe it as 'anthropology without the pain', that is without field research and meticulous analysis.) In other words, there is a considerable overlap between the social sciences, and it may well be argued that the disciplinary boundaries are to some extent artificial. The social sciences represent some of the same interests and try to respond to some of the same questions, although there are also differences. Moreover, anthropology also has much in common with humanities such as literary studies and history. Philosophy has always provided intellectual input for anthropology, and there is a productive, passionately debated frontier area towards biology.

A generation ago, anthropology still concentrated almost exclusively on detailed studies of local life in traditional societies, and ethnographic fieldwork was its main – in some cases its sole – method. The situation has become more complex, because anthropologists now study all kinds of societies and also because the methodological repertoire has become more varied. This book consists in its entirety of a long answer to the question 'What is anthropology?', but for now, we might say that it is *the comparative study of culture and society, with a focus on local life*. Put differently, anthropology distinguishes itself from other lines of enquiry by insisting that social reality is first and foremost created through relationships between persons and the groups they belong to. A currently fashionable concept such as globalisation, for example, has no meaning to an anthropologist unless it can be studied through actual persons, their relationship to each other and to a larger surrounding world. When this level of the 'nitty-gritty' is established, it is possible to explore the linkages between the locally lived world and large-scale phenomena (such as global capitalism or the state). But it is only when an anthropologist has spent enough time crawling on all fours, as it were, studying the world through a magnifying glass, that he or she is ready to enter the helicopter in order to obtain an overview.

Anthropology means, translated literally from ancient Greek, the study of humanity. As already indicated, anthropologists do not have a monopoly here. Besides, there are other anthropologies than the one described in this book. Philosophical anthropology raises fundamental questions concerning the human condition. Physical anthropology is the study of human pre-history and evolution. (For some time, physical anthropology also included the study of 'races'. These are no longer scientifically interesting since genetics has disproven their existence, but in social and cultural anthropology, race may still be interesting as a social construction, because it remains important in many ideologies that people live by.) Moreover, a distinction, admittedly a fuzzy one, is sometimes drawn between *cultural* and *social* anthropology. Cultural anthropology is the term used in the USA (and some other countries), while social anthropology traces its origins to Britain and, to some extent, France. Historically, there have been certain differences between these traditions – social anthropology has its foundation in sociological theory, while cultural anthropology is more broadly based – but the distinction has become sufficiently blurred not to be bothered with here. In the following, the distinction between social and cultural anthropology will only be used when it is necessary to highlight the specificity of North American or European anthropology.

As a university discipline, anthropology is not a very old subject – it has been taught for about 100 years – but it has raised questions which have been formulated in different guises since antiquity: Are the differences between peoples inborn or learned? Why are there so many languages, and how different are they really? Do all religions have something in common? Which forms of governance exist, and how do they work? Is it possible to rank societies on a ladder according to their level of development? What is it that all humans have in common? And, perhaps most importantly: What kind of creatures are humans; aggressive animals, social animals, religious animals or are they, perhaps, the only self-defining animals on the planet?

Every thinking person has an opinion on these matters. Some of them can hardly be answered once and for all, but they can at least be asked in an accurate and informed way. It is the goal of anthropology to establish as detailed a knowledge as possible about varied forms of human life, and to develop a conceptual apparatus making it possible to compare them. This in turn enables us to understand both differences and similarities between the many different ways of being human. In spite of the enormous variations anthropologists document, the very existence of the discipline proves beyond doubt that it is possible to communicate fruitfully and intelligibly between different forms of human life. Had it been impossible to understand culturally remote peoples, anthropology as such would have been impossible; and nobody who practises anthropology believes that this is impossible (although few believe that it is possible to understand everything). On the contrary, different societies are made to shed light on each other through comparison.

The great enigma of anthropology can be phrased like this: All over the world, humans are born with the same cognitive and physical apparatus, and yet they grow into distinctly different persons and groups, with different societal types, beliefs, technologies, languages and notions about the good life. Differences in innate endowments vary within each group and not between them, so that musicality, intelligence, intuition and other qualities which vary from person to person, are quite evenly distributed globally. It is not the case that Africans are 'born with rhythm', or that northeners are 'innately cold and introverted'. To the extent that such differences exist, they are not inborn. On the other hand, it is true that particular social milieux stimulate inborn potentials for rhythmicity, while others encourage the ability to think abstractly. Mozart, a man filled to the brim with musical talent, would hardly have become the world's greatest composer if he, that is a person with the same genetic code as Mozart, had been born in Greenland. Perhaps he would only have become a bad hunter (because of his famous impatience).

Put differently, and paraphrasing the anthropologist Clifford Geertz, all humans are born with the potential to live thousands of different lives, yet we end up having lived only one. One of the central tasks of anthropology consists of giving accounts of some of the other lives we could have led.

ENLIGHTENMENT AND EVOLUTIONISM

This is not the place for a detailed account of the history of anthropology, but a brief excursion back in time is necessary in order to give a proper context to the present and the recent past.

Like other human sciences, anthropology emerged as a distinct field of enquiry in Europe following the period of heightened intellectual awareness and scientific curiosity known as the Enlightenment, at the end of the eighteenth century. More or less trustworthy accounts about remote peoples had already been recorded for centuries by European missionaries, officers and other travellers, and they now formed the raw material for general theories about cultural variation. (An early theory, sometimes attributed to Montesquieu, explained cultural differences as a consequence of climatic variation.) From the mid-nineteenth century onwards, a family of theories usually described as *evolutionism* became dominant. The adherents of these doctrines assumed that societies could be ranked according to their level of development, and unsurprisingly built on the premise that the author's own society was the end-product of a long and strenuous process of social evolution. Technological elements such as the bow and arrow, plough-driven agriculture with beasts of burden and writing were posited as the boundaries between the 'evolutionary levels'. The evolutionist models were both compatible with (and similar in form to) Darwin's theory of biological evolution, which was launched in 1859, and with the colonial ideology stating that non-European peoples must be governed and developed from above, sternly and with force if need be.

Towards the end of the nineteenth century, evolutionist accounts met serious competition in *diffusionism*, a largely German language tendency which, as the name suggests, emphasised the study of the spreading of cultural traits. Whereas the evolutionists tended to assume that every society contained the germ of its own development, diffusionists argued that change largely took place through contact and 'borrowing'.

Momentous changes characterised western societies during the first decades of the twentieth century, with the First World War as a dramatic high point. In the same period, a near total revolution took place in anthropology. The established evolutionist and diffusionist explanations were discarded for several reasons.

Evolutionism was now judged as a fundamentally flawed approach. The increasingly detailed and nuanced studies which were now at the anthropologists' disposal did not indicate that societies developed along a predetermined pattern, and the normative assumption that the scholar's own society was at the top of the ladder had been exposed as plain bigotry and prejudice. The considerable cultural differences between societies possessing roughly the same technology (such as San in southern Africa and Australian Aborigines), indicated that it was unthinkable that 'primitive peoples' could be seen as suggestive of what our own societies might have been like at an earlier stage, which evolutionists claimed.

Diffusionism was rejected chiefly because it made assumptions about contacts and processes of diffusion which could not be substantiated. The fact that similar phenomena, such as techniques or beliefs, existed in two or more places, did not in itself prove that there had been historical contact between them. The phenomenon in question might have developed independently in several places. On the other hand, nobody doubts that diffusion takes place (it is in fact a central premise for a contemporary trend in social science, namely globalisation studies), and it may well be argued that the 'Young Turks' of early twentieth-century anthropology overdid their critique of diffusionism, with the result that anthropology became lopsided in the opposite way; as the study of single, small-scale societies.

Be this as it may, the main point is that the collection of data about 'other cultures' was by now – the decade preceding the First World War – subjected to ever stricter quality demands, and as far as the people who did the collecting were concerned, professional researchers gradually replaced other travellers, going on lengthy expeditions to collect detailed and often specialised data.

THE FOUNDING FATHERS

Four men are conventionally mentioned as the founders of modern anthropology: Franz Boas, Bronislaw Malinowski, AR Radcliffe-Brown and Marcel Mauss. Boas, born in 1864, was German, but emigrated to the USA after several lengthy stays in the country in the 1880s and 1890s. As a professor at Columbia University, he was instrumental in establishing American cultural anthropology, and 'Papa Franz' was the undisputed leader of the discipline until his death in 1942. Most of the American anthropologists of note in the first half of the twentieth century had been students of Boas.

Boas had very wide-ranging interests, but in this context, we shall associate him with two particularly important, and typical, concepts, which contributed to defining American anthropology: *cultural relativism* and *historical particularism*. Cultural relativism is the view that every society, or every culture, has to be understood on its own terms, from within, and that it is neither possible nor particularly interesting to rank societies on an evolutionary ladder.

In Boas' youth, evolutionist perspectives were widespread. In order to understand cultural variation, he argued, this way of thinking is not satisfactory. In fact, he regarded the belief that certain societies were objectively more advanced than others as an ethnocentric fallacy, that is a view governed by prejudice and an unconsidered belief in the superiority of one's own culture.

Cultural relativism is primarily a method (not a world-view) designed to explore cultural variation as independently as possible from the researcher's prejudices. Its aim is to learn to see the world, as far as possible, in the same way as the informants, or 'natives', see it. Theoretical analysis can begin only when this is achieved. In today's public debates about cultural contact and 'integration' of migrants in the West, a similar ideal might be posited; only when one has understood the lives of others, can it be justified to make moral judgements about them.

Boas' historical particularism, which is closely related to cultural relativism, consists of the view that every society has its own, unique history, which is to say that there are no 'necessary stages' that societies pass through. As a result, it is impossible to generalise about historical sequences; they are all unique. All societies have their own paths towards sustainability and their own mechanisms of change, Boas argued. Both this view and certain forms of cultural relativism have always been controversial among anthropologists, but they have been deeply influential up to the present.

Malinowski, born in 1884, was a Pole who studied in Krakow, but he emigrated to England to further his studies in anthropology. Malinowski was a charismatic and inspiring teacher in his time, but his sustained influence has been particularly strong regarding intensive fieldwork as method. Malinowski was not the first to carry out long-term fieldwork in local communities (Boas, for one, had done it), but his study of the inhabitants of the Trobriand islands during the First World War was so detailed and thorough that it set a standard which has its defenders even today. Through a series of books about the Trobriands, the first and most famous of which was *Argonauts of the Western Pacific*, Malinowski showed the enormous intellectual potential of the slow, meticulous and painstakingly detailed study of a small group of which his fieldwork was an exemplar. He wrote about the economy, the religion and the political organisation of the Trobrianders with great authority, and due to his very comprehensive knowledge of their way of life, he was able to demonstrate the interconnections between such partial systems.

In his field methodology, Malinowski strongly emphasised the need to learn the native language, and recommended that the main method should be one of *participant observation*: the ethnographer should live with the people he studied, he should participate in their everyday activities, and make systematic observations as he went along. Similar if not necessarily identical ideals guide anthropological fieldwork even today.

It would be grossly misleading to claim that anthropological investigations began with Boas and Malinowski. Of course, people have asked questions concerning cultural variation and 'how others live' for thousands of years, and both cultural theory and ethnography had existed in various guises long before them. Yet they contributed, perhaps more than anyone else, to turning anthropology into a body of knowledge sufficiently organised and coherent to deserve the label science. The method of fieldwork through long-term participant observation ensured that the knowledge procured by ethnographers was reliable and usable in comparisons, and the principle of cultural relativism was intended not only to keep prejudices in check, but also to develop a neutral, descriptive terminology for describing cultural variation.

Although hardly of central importance, the biographies of Boas and Malinowski may shed a little light on their unorthodox approaches to cultural variation. As indicated above, both men spent most of their adult life abroad; the German Boas in the USA, the Pole Malinowski in England. One may wonder if the uprootedness and alienness they must have felt, both in relation to their native countries and towards their new ones, could not have been a valuable resource when they set out to develop their new science. For it is only when one is able to see one's own culture from a marginal vantage point that one can understand it in anthropological terms. Most people live their entire lives without reflecting upon the fact that they are profoundly shaped by a particular culture. Such 'homeblindness' by default makes them less suited for studying other peoples than those who have realised that even their own habits and notions are created in a particular social environment, under special circumstances; and that they would in crucial ways have been different individuals if they had been raised elsewhere. This kind of reflexivity – self-reflection – is both a condition for the comparative study of culture and society, and a result of it. When the novice anthropologist returns from her first fieldwork, she inevitably views her own society in a new light. However, one must also, to some extent, be able to leave one's own society behind mentally before embarking on fieldwork. Anthropologists try to impart this skill through their teaching of anthropological concepts and models, but the students are unlikely to realise that they have acquired it until it has become too late to return to an earlier state of innocence.

In fact, a significant number of anthropologists have a personal background which has to a certain degree alienated them in relation to their society; quite a few have spent several years in another country as children of diplomats, aid workers or missionaries; some are adopted from another country or have a minority background; and Jews have always been strongly represented in the profession. Women have always been more prominent in anthropology than in most other academic professions. For once, in other words, being a partial stranger can be an asset.

The third of the leading anthropologists during the crucial first decades of the twentieth century was never the less a native Englishman, AR Radcliffe-Brown (1881–1955). Radcliffe-Brown, who spent many years teaching and undertaking research at the universities of Chicago, Cape Town and Sydney, before returning to a chair in Oxford in 1937, is chiefly known for his ambitious scientific programme for social anthropology. Unlike Boas, and to some extent Malinowski, Radcliffe-Brown's interest was not in culture and meaning, but in the ways societies functioned. He was deeply influenced by Emile Durkheim's sociology, which was primarily a doctrine about social integration, and used it as a stepping-stone to develop *structural-functionalism* in anthropology. This theory argued that all the parts, or institutions, of a society filled a particular function, roughly in the same way as all bodily parts contribute to the whole; and that the ultimate goal of anthropology consisted in establishing 'natural laws of society' with the same level of precision as the ones found in natural science. Like Boas and Malinowski, Radcliffe-Brown had his circle of outstanding, devoted students, some of them among the most influential British anthropologists of the postwar years. However, his original programme was eventually abandoned by most of them. It would soon become clear that societies were much less predictable than cells and chemical compounds.

To many anthropologists, the fourth ancestor to be mentioned here is the most important one. Marcel Mauss (1872–1950) is not associated with a concept such as cultural relativism, a method like participant observation, or a theory such as structural-functionalism. Yet his influence on anthropology, especially in France, has been decisive. Mauss was a nephew of the great Durkheim, and they collaborated closely until Durkheim's death in 1917, writing, among other things, a book entitled *Primitive*

Classification together. Mauss was a learned man, familiar with many languages, global cultural history and the classics. Although he never carried out fieldwork, he wrote insightful essays covering a broad range of themes (and relentlessly taught techniques of observation): on the concept of the person in different societies, on nationalism and on the body as a social product. His most famous contribution is a powerful essay about gift exchange in traditional societies. Mauss shows that *reciprocity*, the exchange of gifts and services, is the 'glue' that ties societies together in the absence of a centralised power. Gifts may appear to be voluntary, but are in fact obligatory, and they create debts of gratitude and other social commitments of considerable scope and duration. Other anthropologists continue to build analyses on this perspective even today.

Slightly simplistically, one may say that these four founders and their many students defined the mainstream of twentieth-century anthropology. (Several fascinating minor lines of intellectual descent also exist, but space does not permit an exploration of them here.) However, anthropology has always been a self-critical subject, and these great men did not only exert influence through their admonitions and writings, but also by provoking contradiction and criticism. The cultural relativism of Boas (and the Boasians) met strong resistance in the postwar years, when a new generation of American anthropologists would return to the pre-Boasian concerns with social evolution and concentrate on material conditions, technology and economics. Malinowski, and to some extent his students, were criticised for being unfocused and theoretically weak. Radcliffe-Brown, on his part, was criticised for seeming to believe that his elegant models were more truthful than the far more chaotic social reality; and in France, Mauss was, some years later, largely seen as irrelevant by young, politically radical anthropologists who were more keen on studying conflict than integration.

In the decades after the Second World War, anthropology grew and diversified rapidly. New theoretical schools and perspectives appeared, fieldwork was carried out in new areas, which also added complexity and perspectives; new research centres and university departments were founded, and at the start of the twenty-first century, there are thousands of professional anthropologists worldwide, all of them specialised in one way or another. It may still be said that underneath this teeming diversity, there is a clearly defined, shared subject. The reason is that we continue to return to the same fundamental questions, which are raised in roughly the same ways everywhere. A Brazilian anthropologist and her Russian colleague may perfectly well understand each other (provided they have a common language, which in most cases would be English); there is much to distinguish a feminist postmodernist from a human ecologist, but if they are both anthropologists, they still have much in common intellectually. In spite of intellectual patricides and matricides, heated controversies and bewildering specialisation, anthropology is still delineated through its consistent interest in the relationship between the unique and the universal, its emphasis on 'the native's point of view' (Malinowski's term) and the study of local life, its ambition to understand connections in societies and its comparisons between societies.

FURTHER READING

Barnard, Alan (2000) *History and Theory in Anthropology*. Cambridge: Cambridge University Press.

Kuper, Adam (1996) *Anthropology and Anthropologists: The Modern British School*, 3rd edition. London: Routledge and Kegan Paul.

2
The Key Concepts

The world, as it is perceived by human beings, is to a certain extent shaped by language. However, there is no agreement as to just what the relationship between language and non-linguistic reality is. In the 1930s, the 'Sapir-Whorf hypothesis' was launched by two linguistically oriented anthropologists. The hypothesis proposes that language creates decisive differences between the respective life-worlds different groups inhabit. Certain North American languages – the Hopi language is the most famous example – contained, according to Edward Sapir and Benjamin Lee Whorf, few nouns or words denoting things, and many verbs or words denoting movement and process. As a result, they reasoned, the Hopi world must contain fewer objects and more movement than, say, the life-world typically inhabited by someone who spoke English. This view, which has many adherents (albeit always in a modified form), has been challenged by the view that humans everywhere generally perceive the world in the same ways, and that all languages have many concepts in common.

There is no doubt that when one discusses abstract phenomena, terminology strongly influences what one perceives and how one perceives it. Of course, a Hindu, who is aware of the existence of many divine beings and believes in reincarnation, has ideas about life and death which differ from those of a Muslim, who worships only one god and believes in an eternal, transcendent paradise after death. These ideas are, moreover, likely to inform their everyday lives to a certain extent. In academic studies, similarly, particular concepts enable us to see certain facts in a certain way, at the expense of excluding other aspects of, or approaches to reality. If, for example, one studies a society using kinship as the central concept, one will inevitably discover other connections and problems than one would if one had instead used concepts such as patriarchy or ethnicity.

The choice of concepts and theoretical approaches is influenced both by the researcher's personal interests, his or her training, and – hopefully not least – the society under scrutiny. There is a continuous interaction between theories and concepts, observations and methodological choices, both during and after fieldwork. This will be demonstrated in the next chapter. However, certain concepts are so fundamental to anthropological research that one must relate to them regardless of the topic under scrutiny, and I shall introduce some of them in this chapter, before moving on to research methods and theories.

PERSON

This appears to be a simple and unambiguous word, which everybody understands immediately. Maybe so. However, although everybody knows what a person is, they do not all have the same knowledge. What it is that you see when you look at another human or into the mirror, depends on where you come from. Some of the most inspiring anthropological studies are in fact concerned with revealing exactly these differences; variations in the concept of the person.

In western society, the person is usually perceived as an unique individual, whole and indivisible. During the course of life, the single individual makes a number of individual decisions or choices, and has to take responsibility for their consequences. When someone dies, they cease to exist as individuals, but in western societies, there is no general agreement as to what happens afterwards. Some hold that dead persons somehow continue to live as spiritual beings in an invisible world, while others assume that death is the end of you. The modern western notion of the person is often described as *egocentric*, not in the meaning of egotistic, but as a perspective where the ego, or individual, is at the centre of the stage.

The notion of the person is very different in an Indian village. Most of the population are Hindus and believe in reincarnation, which entails that every newborn baby is a re-born person and not an entirely new one. One is, moreover, not born as an unattached individual, but as a member of a particular caste. Further, one's life is as much decided by one's *karma* and *dharma* (fate, destiny) as by one's own decisions. When someone dies, the cycle of birth, death and rebirth begins anew, and just how someone is reborn depends on their good and bad deeds in this life. This concept of the person is often described as *sociocentric*, which means that it is society or the wider community, not the ego, that is at the centre of the universe.

In African villages where traditional religion is strong, a third conceptualisation of the person can be found. There, persons are typically accorded individual freedom and accountability, but at the same time, the ancestral spirits are present; one may ask them for advice, and one risks being punished by them. Persons who die become ancestral spirits themselves, and in many cases, spiritual mediums (living persons who are able to communicate with the ancestral spirits) can exert considerable secular power.

In parts of Melanesia, to mention a fourth example, yet another conceptualisation of the person is common. Notably, many Melanesians view the transition between life and death in a particular way. The concept of the person tends to be *relational*, which is to say that what constitutes a person is his or her relationships with others. A person who no longer breathes is therefore not considered dead before all his or her relations with others have been brought to an end. Debts must be settled, and certain ritual acts must be carried out, before the person in question is truly dead. Some of the anthropologists who write about India and Melanesia have suggested that, rather than using the term individual, we should speak of the persons in question as *dividuals*, since they are in fact divisible, created through their bonds to other persons.

Gender can be seen as a key term in itself, but it may also be dealt with as a particular instance of the concept of the person, since it is difficult, not to say impossible, to think about a person without gender. Of all the social distinctions that exist, none is more universal than gender. Put differently; all peoples distinguish between men and women, and the gender relationship is an essential element in the constitution of the person everywhere. Men can only be men in relation to women; women are only women in contrast to men. Thus far gender is universal. But just as the general concept of the person varies, gender is understood and dealt with in many different ways.

It is customary to distinguish between sex and gender, although the distinction has gone somewhat out of fashion in some quarters (where the biological component of gender is questioned). Sex generally refers to inherited differences in body size, shape of the genitals and so on; gender is concerned with the social construction of male/female distinctions. In this latter area, that is the subject matter for social scientists who study the topic, there are interesting variations (and, some would argue, just as interesting similarities). The division of labour between men and women varies enormously both in the sphere of production and in the private sphere, and in many societies, gender relations have changed dramatically only in the last 50 years. In most western societies, the majority of women were housewives or part time workers in the 1950s, while the majority are now fully employed outside the home. European and North American men who became fathers in the 1950s and 1960s rarely knew anything about diapers or cooking.

Many social scientists, including anthropologists, have been interested in the power inherent in gender relations, often described through the idiom of female oppression. It can be argued that men usually tend to exert more power over women than *vice versa*. In most societies, men generally hold the most important political and religious positions, and very often, men control the formal economy. In some societies, it may even be prescribed for women to cover their body and face when they appear in the public sphere. On the other hand, women are often capable of exerting considerable informal power, not least in the domestic sphere. Anthropologists cannot state unequivocally that women are oppressed before they have investigated all aspects of their society, including how the women (and men) themselves perceive their situation. One cannot dismiss the possibility that certain women in western Asia (or the Middle East) see the 'liberated' western woman as more oppressed – by professional career pressure, demands to look good and other expectations – than themselves.

When studying societies undergoing change, which perhaps most anthropologists do today, it is important to look at the value conflicts and tensions between different interest groups that are particularly central. Often, these conflicts are expressed through gender relations. In a typical situation, young women, who in contrast to their mothers may be economically self-sufficient, can demand their right to individual freedom within a modern conceptualisation of the person, while the older generation tries to retain their loyalty towards tradition and another, more holistic or sociocentric notion of the person. This kind of conflict is described regularly in the press in western Europe, with reference to immigrant communities, but it can be identified under different guises in many other societies as well.

SOCIETY

This word is used by most social scientists (and others) every day, but they rarely bother to define it. Nor is it easy to do so. In everyday language, the term society tends to be synonymous with 'state'. One speaks of Norwegian society, British society, South African society and so on. But a definition of this kind does not withstand closer scrutiny. First, every state (even the smallest ones) contains several local communities, which may for several purposes be seen as societies in their own right. Moreover, many states are composed of different ethnic groups who speak different languages, who have limited contact and who may have little in common, culturally speaking. Third, the members of society often perceive the state as their enemy (if it is totalitarian), corrupt or they simply feel that it does not represent their interests.

It is perfectly possible to propose a less rigid definition of a society as well. One may, for example, state that a society consists of people who have lived and worked together for a long time, and who therefore feel that they belong to a moral community which obliges them to behave properly towards one another. This kind of definition seems to be more suitable for small communities based on face-to-face interaction than for larger, more abstract societies, and there is nothing wrong with that. After all, societies typically studied by anthropologists have been small. The only problem is that local communities are always part of larger systems; they are dependent on external trade, they may receive their women or their priests from outside, they are perhaps governed more or less efficiently by a remote state administration, the youths may travel back and forth to the big city to work or study, and so on. In this kind of setting, it is impossible to draw a clear and unambiguous boundary around the society.

Such are some of the problems experienced today with the concept of society, notwithstanding certain politicians' statements to the effect that 'there is no such thing as society'. These problems indicate something about the development of anthropology in recent decades, but they also say something about the increasing interconnectedness of the world. In the latter half of the nineteenth century, when many of the current concepts in social science were developed, many of the early sociologists and anthropologists distinguished simply and unceremoniously between two kinds of society: the big and the small; or our own, and all the others. Henry Maine, a lawyer who wrote an important book about 'primitive society' in 1861, distinguished between *status societies* and *contract societies*. In the status society, each person had fixed relationships to others, which were determined by birth, family background and the ensuing rank and position in society. The contract societies were, by contrast, based on voluntary agreements between individuals, and one's standing in society depended on personal achievement, not on birth ascription. Maine regarded contract societies as being more complex than status societies.

Several other theorists who were active in the same period established similar distinctions between small/simple/traditional and large/complex/modern societies. The most influential such distinction is, perhaps, the sociologist Ferdinand Tönnies' contrast between *Gemeinschaft* (community) and *Gesellschaft* (society). The *Gemeinschaft* is a local community where people belong by virtue of shared experiences, based on traditional obligations and personal acquaintance. *Gesellschaft*, on the other hand, is the anonymous large-scale society typical of modernity, where the state and other powerful institutions have largely taken over the roles of family and neighbourhood. In fact, Tönnies wrote about the transition from agrarian to industrial society, and he clearly believed that life in the *Gesellschaft* was governed by a more instrumental, more utilitarian logic of action than the norm-driven, more sociocentric *Gemeinschaft*.

So what is a society? According to Maine, Tönnies and others, we must first of all distinguish between the small and the large, the simple and the complex, those which are based on kinship and reciprocity, and those that are integrated through other mechanisms. Although few anthropologists working after the mid-twentieth century would uncritically adopt a simple dichotomy of this kind, it is clear that many of the societies studied by anthropologists have many elements in common with Tönnies' category of *Gemeinschaft*. On the other hand, many do not, and indicate severe limitations with the categorisation. Indian villages, for example, can be seen both as *Gemeinschaften* and as parts of a larger *Gesellschaft*. In many parts of Africa, traditional social organisation was highly flexible; it expanded and contracted in response to shifting circumstances. Usually, social life would converge on the village, but through trade and conflict, villages were also integrated into larger systems.

Simple dichotomies such as these have long since been abandoned in anthropology. The world is far too complex, and variation between societal types is too vast, for a categorisation dividing it into two mutually exclusive kinds of society to be meaningful. In addition, as argued above, one cannot once and for all draw the boundaries of a society. For this reason, it is more accurate to state that anthropologists, particularly *social* anthropologists, study social life rather than saying that they study societies.

At the same time, it is often both accurate and necessary to regard societies as entities with boundaries. A common criterion for delineating societies is political power. A society, according to this view, is an assemblage of people effectively subjected to the same political apparatus. But even this kind of delineation is problematic. In a modern state, one can claim that the inhabitants in many respects live in the same society. Yet, at the same time, political power is also exerted, to varying degrees, by local government, and several states – not least in Europe – are also integrated in political communities at higher levels. Moreover, in ethnically plural states, the ethnic leadership may sometimes be *de facto* more powerful than the state. Also, there are states, not least in Africa, which are weakly integrated, such that the operational level of political power is located at a lower, more local (often kinship- or locality-based) level. In such cases, the actual power of the state is much less than it may appear on paper.

In spite of the lack of clarity in the concept of society, the word is doubtless necessary. In everyday language, words denoting local communities, large-scale society and global society exist, and all refer to actually existing entities, existing at different systemic levels. Humans are integrated in (that is, they participate in and contribute to) several social systems, some operating at a large scale, others at a small scale. When anthropologists delineate their field of study, the level of scale is determined by the issues at hand. If one is about to do a study of witchcraft among the

Zulu, one delineates the system in a particular way; if the focus of the study is the legal system of South Africa, another delineation is necessary; and if the topic is the relationship between Zulus and Afrikaners, a third social system becomes relevant. All of these partial systems (and many others) exist, and all may be seen as societies.

CULTURE

The third concept to be discussed is just as important as the two previous ones, and it is not easier to grasp. Some would actually argue that the concept of culture is the single most difficult term in anthropology. In 1952, AL Kroeber and Clyde Kluckhohn published the book *Culture: A Critical Review of Concepts and Definitions*, which gave an overview of extant definitions of culture in the discipline. They identified 162 different definitions. Some were, admittedly, quite similar, but they had to conclude that there does not exist a definition of the culture concept that most anthropologists seem to agree upon.

Quite often, the term culture is used as a synonym for society, as when one speaks, in everyday language, about 'other cultures'. At the same time, a view distinguishing the two also seems widespread, as in terms such as 'multicultural society'. If such societies exist, it is in other words possible to have one society, but several cultures. Although this way of speaking can be meaningful in the simplified terminology of journalism and colloquial speech, it is too inaccurate to be useful in anthropological research, even if terms such as 'multicultural society' are suggestive of relevant anthropological issues.

One of the oldest and most famous definitions of culture stems from the English anthropologist EB Tylor, who defined culture as follows on the first page of his book *Culture*, published in 1871: 'Culture or Civilization, taken in its widest ethnographic sense, is that complex whole which includes knowledge, belief, art, morals, custom, and any other capabilities and habits acquired by man as a member of society'. Many have seen this definition as a rather useful one, in spite of – or perhaps because of – its very wide and general character. Tylor includes every 'capability and habit' he can think of, and then some, in his concept of culture. Later attempts at defining culture in the anthropological sense of the word have been less wide-ranging. The leading spokesman for interpretive anthropology, Clifford Geertz, suggested in the 1960s that culture be seen as shared meanings expressed through public communication. Shared culture does not, in other words, entail that everybody has obtained exactly the same knowledge and acquired exactly the same skills, but that those who share a culture also share a world-view and speak the same language in both a literal and a metaphoric sense.

Culture, thus understood, permeates all human activity. Some may still think that economics and politics have little to do with culture; economics is about utility, and politics is about power. But of course, such a description would be unforgivably simplistic. Cultural values, which differ, determine which valuables are perceived as desirable in the economic life of a society, and cultural circumstances regulate the behaviour of political elites. Culture is an *aspect* of human activity, not merely a *sector*.

Most of those who feel comfortable with the concept of culture use it in ways that have more in common with Geertz' definition than with Tylor's. But it must be admitted that the situation is more complicated than it may appear so far. The concept of culture is even more controversial than the concept of society, and it has been criticised for many years by anthropologists who are convinced that they would be better off without it (which I suspect they won't, but see Adam Kuper's *Culture*, 1999, for a different conclusion). The critique of the concept of culture has become a fairly standard exercise in parts of anthropology, and a small cluster of arguments are presented again and again in the literature, ranging from MA dissertations to monographs. In fact, it seems possible to limit the number of core arguments to four.

The first objection concerns the pluralisation of the word; *cultures*. On the one hand, culture can be conceptualised as the opposite of nature. According to this view, all people are equally cultured; it is culture i.e. everything that is learned, such as language, religion and so on, that makes us human, and culture accordingly unites humanity. On the other hand, culture may be used in the plural, and suddenly, culture appears as something which divides humanity instead of uniting it. The attention is shifted from the uniquely human to that which makes groups different from each other.

This way of conceptualising culture was dominant in anthropology throughout the twentieth century, not least because of Boas' cultural relativism and Malinowski's field methodology, focusing as it did on the single society. Some anthropologists, more interested in similarities than in differences, wish to return to an understanding of culture seen as that which unites humanity. According to this view, the actual expressions of culture are obviously unique and variable, but at a deeper level, they refer to something universal.

Objection number two concerns the problem of delineation, and it has much in common with criticisms of the concept of society. Within every human group, however delineated, there is considerable variation, and it is rarely easy to see what are the systematic differences between groups. In some respects, the variations *within* a group can be greater than the variations between groups. This simple point can easily be supported by observation, not least in modern, complex societies. In certain respects, the urban middle classes in western Europe can be said to have more in common with each other than with people from remote parts of their own countries. Moreover, immigration has brought with it a new kind of cultural dynamics, which creates new mixtures of impulses deriving from a variety of sources. The children of immigrants, who have grown up in the new country, may speak Punjabi at home and German outside the home, and draw on a cultural repertoire which is neither Pakistani nor German, but both.

A third example could take the impact of commercial mass culture as its point of departure. Adolescents from all over the world acquire some of the same cultural references since, among other things, they listen to similar music and have seen the same (mostly American) films; and one cannot take it for granted that they share those references with the parental generation. The contemporary world is teeming with mixed cultural forms and transnational flows of cultural elements, which makes it more difficult than ever before to draw boundaries between cultures. Among the many anthropologists who have described culture as a flowing, dynamic process rather than a static and thinglike entity, Ulf Hannerz (1992) is among the most influential. He regards culture as a global web of networks with no absolute boundaries, but adds that the network has its nodes (or 'switchboards') and zones of varying density, and that there simultaneously exist cultural universes, or partial universes, which remain relatively stable and spatially localised.

The third objection concerns the *political* use of the concept of culture. It has become increasingly clear that the classic anthropological concept of culture – that of cultural relativism – has been used to promote particular group claims, to discriminate against minorities and to defend exclusion through aggressive nationalism. This use of the culture concept, which reduces the existing complexity of a society to a few simple categories, has inspired many politically self-conscious anthropologists to scrutinise their own culture concept in an especially critical way. The most famous (and possibly the most extreme) example of a political use of the classical culture concept is the South African apartheid system.

From 1948 to 1994, the South African state practised a politics of *apartheid* (which means apartness in Afrikaans), which aimed to ensure that different peoples did not mix uncontrollably. An ultimate aim of apartheid was to establish separate states based on race, ethnicity and assumed culture. The background of apartheid was the desire among a large part of the white minority to dominate the black majority economically without having to give them equal rights and opportunities; but the ideological justification of the system had uncanny resemblances to cultural relativism. In fact, several South African anthropologists were among the most outspoken defenders of the system, and the main intellectual architect behind the system, Werner Eiselen, was a professor of anthropology. (In the name of justice, it must be added that many South African anthropologists were outspoken critics of the system.) The ideology behind apartheid was unconvincing for many reasons, among them the fact that the various groups had already inhabited the same areas and had influenced each other culturally for centuries. Millions of black South Africans were forcibly moved to so-called homelands from the 1950s, and it was claimed that this physical segregation was for their own good since they could only retain their own culture if they lived in their own, culturally independent space. Apartheid was unique in that it connected a cultural relativist ideology to a brutally oppressive state, but the fact is that the classical Boasian concept of culture can easily be used to defend both ethnic prejudices and nationalism. This discovery has led to a widespread uneasiness concerning the concept of culture, and it has strengthened the case for those who advocate objection number two (the problem of boundaries, internal variation and change).

The fourth and final objection to be mentioned here concerns the inaccurate and lumpy character of the culture concept. Although it has been narrowed down somewhat since Tylor and Boas, the culture concept still appears very wide and vague. Often, culture is invoked to explain conflicts and problems in the media and everyday discourses. If parents beat their children, one might perhaps shrug and say that 'it is their culture'; if fishermen in a particular village splash a few drops of rum on the ground before they go out to sea, they do it because of 'their culture'; if a particular ethnic group is over-represented in the crime statistics, it can be tempting to explain it by referring to 'their culture', and if a voluntary organisation stages a parade with West African music and folk dress, commentators may say that they do it because it 'celebrates their culture'. Many other examples could have been added. The point is that in order to understand what goes on in the world, we need a finer and more nuanced terminology than that which the concept of culture can offer alone. It is far too simple, and it gives an illusion of insight rather than real understanding, to explain events by using the term 'culture' glibly. An alternative consists in using more specific terms instead of speaking loosely about culture. If one speaks of childrearing (primary socialisation), one might *say* childrearing; if one speaks about folk religion, one may say it instead of using the catch-all term culture; and if one really wants to understand variable crime rates within a complex population, it is inconceivable that the term 'culture' offers an adequate explanation.

In spite of the obvious good sense of all the objections presented above, there may be sound reasons to try to save 'culture'. It is beyond doubt that there are relevant, systematic and sometimes striking differences between persons and groups, and that some of these differences – possibly some of the most important ones – are caused by the fact that they have grown up in systematically different social environments. At the outset of this chapter, the divisive potential of language was discussed briefly, but other differences of equal magnitude could also have been mentioned. Although it is necessary to be conscious of variation, the problem of boundaries, political misuse, change, flows and conceptual inaccuracy, it would be tantamount to intellectual suicide for anthropology if it were to discard a concept that tells us that people with different backgrounds, who have been raised in very different environments, live – to a greater or lesser extent – in different life-worlds and see the world in different ways. Thus, it seems necessary to keep the culture concept, but in an ideal world, it would be locked securely up in a cupboard and taken out only when it was needed. In most cases where the culture concept is used cursorily today – inside and outside of anthropology – it would prove unnecessary to unlock the cupboard.

TRANSLATION

A crucial task for anthropology, and one of the most demanding ones, consists in translation, and this refers not just to verbal translation from one language to another; just as important is the translation of non-verbal acts. It is obvious that translation can be difficult. Even translation between written versions of closely related languages such as English and German can be problematic. If one then moves to a society which is radically different from one's own and tries to describe what the inhabitants say and do in one's own language, it stands to reason that there are many difficulties to be resolved.

Although anthropologists both engage in conversation and observe interaction on fieldwork, it is common practice to begin by learning the meaning of native terms and concepts. This is not just because it is important in itself to understand language, but also because native terms are used locally to describe acts. In order to understand a ritual in an Asian village community, for example, it is not sufficient to observe what the actors do; one must also learn the meaning and connotations of the words they use to describe it. This sounds trivial and obvious, but in fact a depressing number of people believe they have understood a phenomenon when they have 'seen it with their own eyes'. Anthropologists have higher demands, and insist that we have only understood a phenomenon when we are able to understand and explain, as far as possible, what it signifies to the local population.

Some readers will have noticed the use of the term 'native' above. The word seems dated, perhaps even condescending. The way it is used by contemporary anthropologists, it is neither. Italians are just as 'native' as the inhabitants of a Pacific island.

A characteristic native term in Norwegian is *fred og ro*, which translates into English as 'peace and quiet'. However, in native usage in Norway the concept of *fred og ro* has particular cultural connotations which entail that a direct translation is not sufficient to cover its whole meaning. Cultural translation thus implies that one accounts for the full meaning of native concepts, indicating their usage and scope. It does not, therefore, limit itself to translation of single concepts, but also shows how they are connected with other concepts, and ultimately how they form a continuous whole, i.e. a cultural universe.

Sometimes, anthropologists may come across concepts (or acts) that seem untranslatable. For example, it has been argued that certain peoples do not distinguish between thoughts and emotions in the way that one does in European languages, but instead use one term which could be glossed roughly as 'thought-feeling'. In such cases, it may be necessary to use the native term in the anthropological account, without translating it. This reminds us that the world is being partitioned in ways which can vary significantly. Even two geographically neighbouring languages such as English and Welsh distinguish between green and blue in different ways; certain nuances are perceived as blue in English, but green in Welsh. Even 'objective', universally human things such as body parts are not delineated in the same ways by all people. An Argentine butcher cuts up a carcass along other lines than a German one and uses a vocabulary to describe the kinds of beef which overlaps only partly with the German; similarly, the boundaries between human body parts are not the same everywhere. The Ibo in Nigeria, for example, use a single term to denote the entire leg, from the foot to the thigh.

These kinds of translation problems are never the less relatively simple and straightforward. It is far more difficult to translate abstract terms, i.e. concepts about spirits, moral values, abstract systems of classification and so on. In his magisterial book about the religion of the Nuer, a Sudanese cattle people, EE Evans-Pritchard (1956) describes their beliefs and religious concepts in great detail, and takes great pains to depict their spiritual world, notions about the afterlife and rituals in the way they are perceived by the Nuer themselves. The book is highly regarded and is often on the reading list in courses on the anthropology of religion, and yet it has been suggested that Evans-Pritchard's cultural translation may have been coloured by his own beliefs, as he was a Catholic. In particular, it has been claimed that the creative spirit among the Nuer, *kwoth*, is described in a way that makes it resemble the Christian god.

All cultural translation necessitates some interpretation and simplification. No sane reader would be able to make sense of a text which consisted exclusively of directly translated, unmediated quotations from informants. *Compression* and *editing* are therefore necessary elements of cultural translation. Moreover, no matter how outstanding an anthropologist is, as a fieldworker, as a writer and as an analyst, the text always represents a selection, and it will always to a greater or lesser extent be marked by the subjectivity of the translator.

In other words, it appears impossible to achieve a 'pure' cultural translation; the text will always be influenced by the anthropologist's professionally specific interests. The questions that are pressing for anthropologists in their research on remote (or not so remote) people, are not necessarily the same issues as the ones the natives are interested in. They also use their abstract concepts (such as gender, class, ethnicity, hierarchy, etc.) to organise the data, and corresponding concepts do not always exist in the life-worlds of the informants.

The only final solution to the problem of translation, seen as the spectre of misrepresentation, seems to be to allow the informants to speak without interruption, that is to function as their microphone stand. Such an extreme approach, where the outcome would inevitably be a series of long, unmediated and unedited monologues, would show, at the most, how important the anthropologist's interpretation, compression and editing is. Such text would be incomprehensible and unreadable. Besides, translation does not just consist of making verbal utterances comprehensible, but also in explaining patterns of action and principles of social organisation.

No cultural translation is perfect and definite, and all translations have an element of subjectivity, but there are criteria for distinguishing the good from the bad. Superficial translations can often be recognised by their lack of context and therefore do not convince the qualified reader. Misunderstandings and simple mistranslations can also often be discovered by consulting other sources, such as other anthropologists who have worked in the area. The anthropologist, moreover, should not seem either too close to or too distant from the people she or he writes about. Too great a degree of closeness, as when one writes about 'one's own people', can lead to *homeblindness*, that is a failure to observe essential features of a society due to the fact that one takes it for granted. Too great a distance may imply that the anthropologist becomes unable to grasp 'the native's point of view' to a sufficient degree. The art of cultural translation consists in oscillating between distance and nearness, between one's own concepts and the native ones, or – to put it differently – making the exotic familiar and the familiar exotic.

COMPARISON

Most anthropologists agree that comparison is an important part of what they do, but there are many views as to what kinds of comparison are possible and/or desirable. Before moving on, we must be clear about the aim of comparison. It does not consist in ranking societies or cultures according to their 'level of development' or moral qualities. Comparison is a means to clarify the significance of the anthropologist's findings, through creating contrasts, revealing similarities with other societies, and to develop (or criticise) theoretical generalisations.

In everyday language, it is often said that 'one cannot compare apples and pears'. If by this one means that certain things cannot be compared because they are qualitatively different, such as a tin of olives and a book of poetry, the admonition may be relevant. If, however, it means that phenomena that are very different, such as the division of labour on a Pacific island and in a town in the USA, cannot be compared, many anthropologists would disagree. The aim of comparison is to understand differences just as much as similarities, and as long as there are enough similarities to make particular comparisons possible, the job may be worth undertaking.

So what is it that anthropologists do when they make comparisons? First of all it must be made clear that comparison takes place continuously in anthropological writing, and some distinctions are necessary. First, translation itself is a form of comparison; we implicitly compare the native language, its concepts and so on with our own through translation. Second – and now we are talking about translation with a conscious purpose – anthropologists compare through establishing contrasts and similarities between societies or other entities that they study. Evans-Pritchard once said that his studies of witchcraft among the Azande in Central Africa made it easier for him to understand the Soviet Union under Stalinism. In both societies, the fear of being accused of a violation of vaguely defined norms induced most people to try to follow the norms slavishly. More typical comparisons could be undertaken between Indian and western European conceptualisations of the person, briefly discussed above, or the contrast between arranged marriages and love marriages, often dealt with in research (and in journalism) on Asian immigrants in western Europe. Such comparisons try to shed light not only on the institutions under scrutiny, but also on more general features of the societies in question.

Third, comparison is used to investigate the possible existence of human universals. If, for example, it is shown that all human groups possess concepts about the colours red, black and white (which seems to have been proven), we must assume that the ability to distinguish between these colours is an inborn feature of the human species. Comparative studies have also shown that all peoples have concepts, and norms, about incest prohibitions, descent, gender roles and many other social phenomena. The problem with most universals of this kind, however, is that on closer investigation it nearly always becomes apparent that such concepts, when they are translated into local realities, refer to very different phenomena, and one must then ask if the universal is really there, or whether the apparent similarities are created by the comparer, imposing the concepts onto phenomena which are actually very diverse.

Comparison is not just used in attempts, often controversial ones, to identify universals, but also to disprove such claims. An example, to be treated in greater detail later, is the debate about aggression. Many, especially those who are inspired by an evolutionary, biological perspective on humanity, have argued that aggression is an inborn universal, especially prominent among men. Against this view, many anthropologists have claimed, often referring to their own ethnography, that there exist peoples who neither have notions about aggression nor practices that can be described as aggressive. A rejoinder to this argument could in turn be that aggression exists everywhere, but that it may be expressed in different ways which are not necessarily recognisable as aggression to the researcher, such as song duels among the Inuit (Eskimos).

For two reasons, it is impossible to arrive at final answers that everyone can agree on here. Since translation is a necessary condition for comparison, and cultural translation always has an element of uncertainty, it can never be proven strictly and beyond dispute that one actually compares whatever it is that one claims to compare. Besides, comparison always threatens to lead to a degree of decontextualisation – single traits are compared with little attention to the wider context – which may entail misleading results. It may rightly be argued, for example, that although it has been shown that all peoples have a notion of the colour white, it is more relevant to explore the cross-cultural variations in the local understandings of the colour white – to see the whiteness in its full cultural context – than merely to state that whiteness is a native category everywhere. As is well known, whiteness is the colour of mourning in China, sharing at least in this respect the significance of the colour black in Europe.

Fourth, comparison is sometimes spoken of as a 'quasi-experiment' in anthropology. In the laboratory sciences, the experiment is the most important source of new knowledge. An experiment amounts to introducing controlled changes into a setup where one has full knowledge of the relevant variables, mapping out the consequences of the changes. If a group of natural scientists wish to investigate the effects of a hormone, they may take two groups of rats, which are otherwise similar in key respects. Group A is given the hormone, while group B (the control group) gets nothing or an ineffective placebo. If the members of group A on average grow markedly more rapidly than the members of group B, it is reasonable to assume that the hormone promotes growth. An experiment may also be undertaken on a single group, which is observed under changing circumstances over a stretch of time. For the experiment to be reliable, it is necessary that all the variables except the one under investigation are kept constant, which is to say that one only allows variations in the values of the variables whose effects are to be gauged.

In anthropological research, it is impossible to keep single variables constant. If one were to place a group of natives into an artificial, controlled situation, the resulting interaction would lose the very context that guarantees its authenticity, and the result would be useless. The closest anthropologists get to the methodological ideals of the experiment is therefore through comparison. One would then compare two or several societies with many similarities, but with one or a few striking differences. One would thereby be in a position to account for the differences. In a famous comparison from the 1950s, between some central African societies which had much in common, Siegfried Nadel argued that there was a link between the kinship system, the pattern of settlement and the relative importance of witchcraft. If the kinship system was patrilineal and the pattern of settlement was virilocal (the wife moved in with the husband), witchcraft accusations would most likely be more common – and they would be directed towards the women, who came from outside the village – than in societies where the pattern of settlement followed other principles.

HOLISM AND CONTEXT

The term holism may have connotations of mysticism and fuzzy religiosity. Many religions, not least contemporary syncretisms of the new age kind, offer promises of holistic understanding, holistic healing and so forth. In anthropology, the term is used differently, and refers to a method for describing how single phenomena are connected to other phenomena and institutions in an integrated whole. In classical functionalist anthropology, as in Malinowski, one assumed that entire societies were perfectly integrated, like jigsaws where all the pieces fit and none has fallen behind the couch; and that culture – the symbolic, meaningful superstructure – fits perfectly in the social organisation. This ultrafunctionalist view has long been abandoned. As early as 1954 Edmund Leach showed, in a study of religion and politics among the Kachin of upper Burma, that societies are far from being in an integrated equilibrium. They are unstable, they change, and there are several competing versions of the myths of origin, some of which induce the inhabitants to revolt. An even more radical critique of the idea that the different parts, or institutions, in societies are well integrated with one another came in the 1960s with Fredrik Barth's 'transactionalism', a model of analysis which puts the acting individual at the centre, and which does not assume that social integration is a necessary outcome of interaction.

However, holism does not necessarily mean that societies or cultures hang together in a perfect, logical or functional way. It may also be a way of thinking which assumes that phenomena are connected to other phenomena and create some kind of entity based on interconnections and mutual influence between its various elements, without taking it for granted that this entity should be of a lasting character, or that it encompasses an entire society or an entire population group. A couple of examples might make it clearer what holism can entail in this more modest and flexible sense.

The cultural category of *kastom* in Melanesian pidgin refers to tradition, values, ways of behaving and results of human creativity that the local population regard as local in their origins. In the twentieth century, the Melanesian islands, which stretch from New Guinea to Fiji, were drawn into the world economy; they are now governed by modern state formations, and the populations have to relate to mass media, schools and a monetary economy. The changes have inspired the growth of a widespread *identity politics* among many Melanesian peoples, where they are conscious of the need to retain traditional cultural forms in order to avoid the loss of personal and collective autonomy. The term *kastom* is used to identify social facts that have other origins and another moral basis than the modern. As the Melanesian said to the anthropologist (according to Marshall Sahlins) 'If we didn't have *kastom*, we'd be just like the white man'. The concept refers to a broad range of ideas and ways of life that relate to modernisation in an ambiguous way; it is about resistance, self-assertion and identity, but also about the enduring viability of traditional cultural forms in situations of rapid change. Although it is seen as anti-modern, *kastom* is also a paradoxical, countercultural product of modernity, since it is cast in the idiom of modernity. The 'grammar' of *kastom* resembles traditionalism elsewhere.

A description of *kastom* which shows how it enters into, and engages with, different aspects of society and of social life, is holistic. It does not suggest that these societies are particularly tightly integrated, or that they are particularly stable – on the contrary, Melanesian societies can be rather fragmented and fast-paced – but that singular phenomena can only be fully understood through their internal connections to other phenomena. The use of the headscarf, or *hijab*, among Muslim women in western Europe cannot be understood unless one sees it in the context of local labour markets and media, as well as postcolonial identity politics in the non-dominant world as such.

In a description of Norwegian cultural forms, Eduardo Archetti mentions that when, as a relatively newly arrived immigrant in the country in the 1970s, he wanted to buy a colleague a cup of coffee in the university canteen, the colleague paid him back the moment he returned from the till with the coffee. The colleague was, in other words, determined to settle his debt immediately.

Seen as an isolated event, the scene is pure anecdote, and although natives would intuitively understand the cause of Archetti's confounded reaction, it contributes little to unpacking Norwegian culture and society for outsiders. But when Archetti sees it in the wider context of Norwegian history and ideology, it can be understood as the expression of a central feature of Norwegian social life. Repaying incurred debts immediately is known as *balanced reciprocity* in anthropology, and the tendency to do so in Norwegian everyday life is a result of a desire to avoid vague and long-lasting debts of gratitude towards people one does not feel familiar with. The logic of balanced reciprocity can be identified in many kinds of situation, and it can be connected both to historical circumstances such as the fact that most Norwegian farmers were independent smallholders (feudalism was weak in this area) and to related Protestant values such as thrift and equality. Archetti associates the immediate 'return gift' with values such as independence and self-sufficiency. A description of balanced reciprocity, so typical of Norwegian everyday life, becomes a holistic one when it reveals the ways in which large clusters of meaning and norms (ideologies) are reflected in and revealed through small, seemingly insignificant events.

Yet another example could be FBD marriage (marriage with father's brother's daughter) as it is practised in North Africa and the Middle East. Seen from western Europe, this custom may appear a bizarre one, bordering on incest and in violation of the individual's right to choose his or her spouse freely. A holistic description of the practice will none the less reveal that it is meaningful and rational within a particular kind of social universe. The societies in question are patrilineal, and property (land and/or herds) is divided among the children when a man dies. A marriage alliance between a man and his father's brother's daughter (FBD) thus signifies an attempt to prevent fragmentation of family property. Moreover, the relation between brothers is strong and politically significant in these societies, which means that a further strengthening of their relationship serves to confirm important social patterns. The kin group is consolidated, and possible conflicts that might arise through intermarriage with other kin groups are avoided. There is, incidentally, no society that proscribes FBD marriage, but in the societies in question, it is considered a good solution if practicable.

Holism in anthropology, thus, entails the identification of internal connections in a system of interaction and communication. The word has gone somewhat out of fashion in recent years, particularly because many anthropologists now believe that they study fragmented worlds which are only integrated in a piecemeal fashion. Never the less, the examples above indicate that holism today is to do with *contextualisation* rather than postulating the existence of tightly integrated and stable entities. In the analytical methodology of anthropologicy, *context* may actually be the key concept. It refers to the fact that every phenomenon must be understood with a view to its dynamic relationship to other phenomena. No forms of belief, technologies, marriage systems or economic practices (to mention a few examples) have any meaning whatsoever unless they are understood in a wider context. If an anthropologist tries to understand Islam, he will not limit himself to studying the Qu'ran, but will also study the life-worlds of Muslims, that is to say their world as it appears from within. If an anthropologist intends to study the Internet, she will presumably carry out research both online and offline. Offline research is necessary in order to learn about the lives of Internet users outside the Internet itself, which in turn helps to make sense of whatever it is they are doing online. The methodological requirement of contextualisation is fundamental in all anthropological research, but as the examples above indicate, every phenomenon has several possible contexts. The choice of relevant contexts is dependent on the priorities of the researchers.

FURTHER READING

Leach, Edmund (1982) *Social Anthropology*. Glasgow: Fontana.
Delaney, Carol (2004) *Investigating Culture: An Experiential Introduction to Anthropology*. Oxford: Blackwell.

3
Fieldwork

The anthropological production of knowledge has at least two elements; fieldwork and analysis. Some might want to add a third one, namely description; one first collects a body of empirical material through various field methods, one then describes whatever it is that one has discovered, and finally, one analyses the findings. Many, including the author, are skeptical of the distinction between description and analysis because the (anthropological) analysis inevitably begins in the (ethnographic) description itself. No all-encompassing, neutral description exists of anything. Already the delineation of the field of enquiry – socially, thematically, with respect to the concepts used – necessarily entails that reality 'out there' is presented in a selective and theoretically biased way. It is impossible to describe everything, or to give equal emphasis to everything one has observed. For example, suppose that it is an unquestionable fact that only men can achieve political power in society X. Nobody has ever heard of a woman holding a formal political position there. At the same time, only men from particular, aristocratic lineages are entitled to compete for these positions. Two academic articles about this society are published. One describes it as a patriarchal system, the other as a feudal one. Both are right, but they throw light on different aspects of the society.

The map is always simpler than the territory. When the map (description and analysis) is drawn up, the person who designs it must decide whether it should be a political or a geological map, which scale to use, which features ought to be included – rivers, mountains, tourist attractions or ocean depths – and how it ought to be bounded, by province, country or continental borders, for example. An anthropologist is faced with analogous decisions. This chapter shows, through examples, how the choices made at different points during the research process lead to different results. Like historical writings, anthropological texts always fuse an element of objectivity with an element of creativity. It is the researcher (and his or her peers, who judge the work critically) who gives a particular form to the chosen segment of reality, and in this respect, the production of anthropological texts is a creative activity.

The central activity in anthropological research method is fieldwork. It is through this method that the subject gets most of its primary data. However, the researcher must have some ideas about the issues at hand before embarking on fieldwork. At a practical and prosaic level, it is usually necessary to write a project proposal in order to get the necessary funding and permits. This proposal normally contains the researcher's *hypotheses*, that is his or her assumptions about the crucial issues in the field under scrutiny. Moreover, it must contain an empirical delineation or a framework for the planned fieldwork. It is impossible to study everything, and it is professionally uninteresting to travel somewhere just in order to find out 'how they live out there'. If one has a weakness for this kind of topic, one might be well advised to write a travel book rather than doing anthropology.

When I left for my first fieldwork in Mauritius early in 1986, I had read much of what had been written about this multi-ethnic island state over the last 200 years. Many of those who plan fieldwork these days are in a less fortunate situation: They must delimit themselves more rigidly before fieldwork. If one intends, say, to study the economic situation of peasants in a Mexican province, it is impossible to read even a fraction of everything that has been written about Mexico beforehand; it is probably not even feasible to read most extant texts about Mexican peasants. One must, thus, choose literature according to assumed relevance. Historical research and archival sources may sometimes be as relevant as recent anthropological studies.

Moreover, it is necessary to read relevant literature from other societies, in order to sharpen one's understanding and, in some cases, in preparation for comparison. In my case, I had to delve into the research about other plantation societies founded by the colonial powers, and as it happened, I found work about Caribbean societies and Fiji to be particularly useful. For the researcher planning Mexican fieldwork, writings about peasants in other parts of Latin America may be relevant, but it could also be fruitful to look at literature dealing with peasants in Africa and eastern Europe.

Finally, it is necessary to prepare theoretically for fieldwork. For my own part, I concentrated in particular on social theory dealing with the relationship between the acting person and social structure, since I was especially interested in the relationship between systemic pressures and agency among villagers of African descent (called Creoles in Mauritius). My central hypothesis was that the (assumed) important ethos of free choice among the Creoles paradoxically led to strong structural coercion as they went about their affairs, since the freedom ethos disabled them from organising collectively and efficiently through formal organisations and interest groups. To the Mexico researcher, a relevant source might be analytical literature about peasant societies and their ties of dependence to the engulfing capitalist economy, and – even more generally – theory about the cultural aspects of economies.

So, following such preparations, one leaves for fieldwork, head chock-full of problems, hypotheses and facts, more often than not with clear assumptions about the characteristics of the field. Often, anthropologists end up doing roughly what the project proposal states that they should do, but it would be untrue to claim that this is always the case. The dynamics of fieldwork are such that initial research plans tend to be modified to a greater or lesser extent. There is a continuous back-and-forth movement between the experiences and data collected in the field, and the researcher's hypotheses and assumptions. For, if one knew exactly what the field looked like and which problems it posed before leaving, and in fact found what one expected at the outset, one might almost have stayed at home. In my case, I quickly realised that there were a couple of issues that were so central in Mauritian everyday life that it would be impossible to neglect them: ethnicity and social change. It soon turned out that very many events in Mauritius are interpreted through an ethnic frame of understanding; if, say, the price of electricity went up, this would be explained locally (in my Creole village) by claiming that the Hindus (who held the political power) did not care about poor, rural Creoles; if one of the adolescent boys in the village was not admitted into his secondary school of choice, the explanation was that the Creoles were deliberately kept back, and so on. As far as social change was concerned, it was impossible to ignore the fact that Mauritius was about to be industrialised and touristified, a double process of economic change which was bound to have consequences for my informants, no matter who they might be. As it happened, I ended up writing a very different dissertation from the one envisioned in the project proposal, namely a study of ethnic relations and multi-ethnic nationhood in a situation of social change, instead of an ethnography of the Creoles.

WHAT IS EMPIRICAL MATERIAL?

The fieldwork itself may proceed in a number of different ways. It has been said that anthropologists cast their net far and wide, working broadly rather than deeply during fieldwork, and pull the threads together only when they transform their fieldnotes into articles and dissertations. This kind of statement is partly correct, but it is also misleading. For with no clear problems (or hypotheses) and delineations, one runs the risk of returning home with a fragmented, far too wide-ranging body of material which can hardly be used for anything but travel writing and party anecdotes. The aim of fieldwork is not to talk to as many people as possible and gather knowledge about as many topics as possible, but to delimit oneself sufficiently to be able to truly master a restricted empirical field. On the other hand, it is also probably correct that ethnographers take notes and record almost everything they see and hear during fieldwork, based on the sound assumption that it is impossible to judge the ultimate relevance of any observation without hindsight.

Frequently, the usefulness of one's observations becomes clear only when one sits down with one's thick bundles of notes, trying to discover or impose patterns, regularities and interconnections in one's often sprawling material. I have supervised students who return from the field with impressive material based on structured interviews with more than 100 persons, only to find out later that the truly important breakthroughs and crucial observations were made during informal gatherings or in situations that were not intended to happen. Since anthropologists do not carry out experiments or try to control their research in other ways, their enterprise may be said to depend on serendipity. And, since the method is unusually time-intensive, fortunate coincidences are in most cases bound to occur sooner or later. Often when one least expects it, things fall into place.

The most important single research method under the umbrella of fieldwork is conventionally spoken of as 'participant observation', following the example of Malinowski. This slightly vacuous term may sound like an oblique admission of not having a method at all. However, the term conceals a variety of precise strategies of data collection, ranging from structured interviewing to lengthy periods of hanging around on the corner. A main goal of participant observation consists of encountering informants in everyday contexts. Rather than pulling people into artificial or 'experimental' situations, the anthropologist observes them, and speaks with them, in their ordinary situations. Instead of interviewing them via questionnaires, anthropologists have long conversations with them, partly on their own terms, in order to obtain their versions of the issues at hand and their reflections about their own existence, rather than concise answers to specific questions. Most anthropologists use other sets of methods as well, and the choice of methodology is influenced by the problems dealt with and the possibilities given by the empirical field. If one's goal is to understand, say, the recreational use of cabins in Scandinavian societies, one will need statistics and historical material about the spread of cabins, as well as contemporary publications aimed at cabin owners. If one's research is about the social implications of AIDS in a South African community, one will need knowledge about the preventive measures taken by the national health authorities, the national profiles of NGOs and so on, in addition to local processes; and if the project is about political Islam in an Indonesian community, it would be necessary to know something about both political culture at the national level in Indonesia and the global Islamic movement as well as the political significance of Pan-Arabism at least since the oil crisis in 1973.

In classic social anthropology, from about 1920 to 1970, most anthropologists carried out their fieldwork in small communities, often villages. Fieldwork typically lasted between one and two years. The anthropologist ideally lived in the village, preferably finding accommodation with a family (or, as in Malinowski's case, 'pitching his tent in the village'), and quickly developed a broad personal network of contacts simply by virtue of being there. In a village, one is bound to become acquainted with 'everybody' whether one tries to or not. The anthropologists would then follow their informants around to the fields or on fishing trips, to religious events, funerals and other rites of passage, to town in order to go to the market; they would spend the evenings with them, would have their meals with them, would learn the language so well that they eventually even understood the jokes; and would speak with the informants about every conceivable matter. As often as it was practically possible, they would take notes and photographs. After the end of fieldwork, the anthropologist would possess a mass of data, and even if he or she was primarily interested in religion and rituals, it would also be necessary to collect data about economics and kinship, since it was a fundamental assumption in classic anthropology that all the institutions of a society were tightly interrelated.

Even then, there were many exceptions to this somewhat idealised description. Many anthropologists (perhaps especially in the French tradition) employed paid, native research assistants, many worked with interpreters, and many preferred to live somewhat more comfortably than village life would have permitted. None the less, village fieldwork was and is a unique opportunity to become deeply familiar with a community and its culture. It enables the anthropologist to get well acquainted with a large number of people and to understand local conditions exceptionally well, since he or she has the same experiences many times over. Village life tends to be repetitive, and besides, it is not methodologically satisfactory to take part in, for example, a funeral only once. For all one knows, this particular funeral might be untypical.

Later, that is after around 1970, other forms of fieldwork increasingly became the norm (they always existed, but formerly as a marginal specialty). Today, it is the rule rather than the exception that anthropologists work in complex societies, where their sets of problems may either require fieldwork in a city or multi-sited fieldwork, and where it may be impossible to cultivate one's relationships with informants for longer periods and/or throughout the day. It is by no means unproblematic to follow people to their working place in a modern society, and far from everybody in such societies would willingly invite an anthropologist to join them in front of the television set in the evening. A number of my students have in recent years studied Internet users, and their contact with their informants has largely been restricted to situations where they actively use the Internet, or cafe encounters. They naturally ask questions about work, family life and leisure, but their opportunity to participate in these spheres is limited. Anthropologists who carry out research on immigrant minorities in multi-ethnic societies often do fieldwork in cities, where most of the immigrants live, and they will frequently use organisations, religious centres, schools or cafes as points of entry into the networks they wish to explore. An increasing number of anthropologists have never visited their informants at home.

The aim of ethnographic research is still to understand local practices and notions in their full context, but large scale and complexity have created new methodological challenges. In complex societies, anthropologists depend less on participant observation than in small-scale communities. They will inevitably relate, albeit selectively, to fiction and mass media, statistics and historical studies, and thereby try to compensate for the lack of continuity in their contact with informants. One runs the continuous risk that the informants, on their part, will prefer to go home and be left alone, or disappear in the middle of fieldwork, or fail to show up for appointments; and it is by no means certain that one will gain access to their social networks.

A main challenge for fieldworkers in complex societies consists of preventing the fragmentation and decontextualisation of their material. Fragmentation entails the collection of scattered, poorly interconnected data; decontextualised data are snippets of knowledge which lack the information needed to connect them to an overarching perspective. If, for example, one has decided to study national and ethnic identity in multi-ethnic Trinidad, it would be relevant to learn that a gardener working for a municipal authority in a small town states that he would not mind if his daughter decides to marry a man from a different ethnic group; but this piece of information is useless unless the reader is given more information about this man, such as his age, his ethnic identity and his family background, where he lives, his religious beliefs and practices, and whether he has any relevant personal idiosyncracies (such as unusual political sympathies) or unusual personal experiences (such as periods spent abroad) that distinguish him from most other Trinidadians.

Regardless of whether one works in a small-scale society or in a large city, ethnographic method requires contextualisation and holism. Every phenomenon deemed relevant must be understood in its full context, and the researcher must indicate its connections with other conditions. Anthropological research is neither particularly capital-intensive nor labour-intensive. It is inexpensive research which rarely demands more advanced equipment than the researcher him- or herself, since most social anthropologists hold that a human being is the most accurate instrument with which to study other humans. This kind of research cannot be said to be very intensive in terms of labour input either, although it can be demanding enough, not least on a personal level. But much of the time, the typical ethnographer is simply chatting with people or waiting for them to turn up.

On the other hand, anthropological research is a characteristically *time-intensive* enterprise. Fieldwork tends to encompass a great deal of trial and error, waiting, misunderstandings, frustrations and boredom, apart from the fact that the anthropologist must necessarily cover the same ground several times in order to ensure that the findings are as accurate as possible. It is common in anthropological research to distinguish between observations and verbal information; that is, what people do and what they say. Anthropologists do not take people's statements at face value; they also wish to observe what they are actually doing. This is not due to an assumption that people are in general notorious liars, but to the fact that statements and acts offer qualitatively different types of material. If one asks an informant what she would do in a given situation, she would give a particular response; but then one may well discover, after a while, that in fact, she does something altogether different. It may also become apparent that one is only able to understand what an informant is saying after observing what she is doing.

The significance of observational data can hardly be exaggerated. Far too many social scientists seem to believe that verbal communication, either via interviews or questionnaires, offers a shortcut to an understanding of people's life-worlds. But it is not always possible to place one's views on a scale ranging from, say, 'I fully agree' to 'I fully disagree'. For my own part,

I have the most advanced social scientific education available, yet whenever I am rung up by a pollster asking where I last saw a particular advertisement or how I evaluate the future of monarchy on a scale from 1 to 5, I rarely know what to say. People's opinions about complex questions, for example how many immigrants they think there ought to be in their home country, can rarely be summarised in a single word (the categories tend to be 'more than', 'fewer than', or 'as many as' the present situation). As everybody knows, with the possible exception of certain social scientists, the answers given to such questions depend on a number of conditions, for example, recent media stories dealing with minority issues – is it, for instance, violent crime among immigrants or ethnic discrimination in the labour market that has made the headline recently? – is it relevant for the kind of answers given, but even more importantly, the perceived context of enquiry is important. There are sound reasons to assume that few inhabitants in more economically developed countries want a large number of 'welfare tourists' from poorer countries to settle; most would in all likelihood be more positively inclined towards giving asylum to persons who have fled persecution in authoritarian societies; and if they are told that increased immigration is necessary for the maintenance of social welfare, an even larger proportion of the population is likely to accept a high immigration rate. Moreover, to many in the West it makes a difference where the immigrants come from; in western countries, there has been a rising antipathy towards Muslims in parts of the population; Africans and other black persons are disliked by others, and yet others hold negative views of particular groups from other European countries.

Instead of a questionnaire survey, one might consider investigating this matter through a series of in-depth interviews. The number of informants would thereby be reduced, but the material would be richer and more nuanced. But even this kind of method has its limitations. This is not primarily because the respondents may be inclined to flatter the researcher by giving the answers they suspect he or she would approve of, but also because there are many questions to which there are no possible, or valid, verbal responses. Many parts of culture are implicit and nonverbal. It may well be that many of those who state that they have positive views of immigrants still avoid sitting next to one on the bus, and routinely avoid shortlisting applicants with 'foreign names' when in a position to do so. They may not be consciously aware of doing so, and it is the task of research to reveal this kind of discrepancy between statements and actions.

Some years ago, a poll firm was appointed to investigate how Norwegians related to the main evening news programme on television. A representative sample was phoned by the pollsters and asked if they had seen the programme that evening. The majority confirmed that they had. The next question concerned whether they could mention at least one of the news stories from the programme they had just seen. Most of the respondents were in fact unable to do so.

This finding is interesting, but it is unclear what it means. At least three alternative interpretations of the material are possible. First, it is possible that many of the respondents lied. They had not seen the evening news, but they wanted to give a good impression to the nice person on the phone. Second, it is conceivable that many *believed* that they had seen the news programme (they usually did, or thought that they usually did). Third – and this is arguably the most interesting possibility – it is possible that they *had* seen the programme, but that it does not function in the way its producers believe it does. In this case, it may be that this and similar news programmes do not primarily give their viewers an opportunity to follow current affairs, but rather constitute the framework for a daily ritual which creates a sense of predictability and security as well as a pretext for taking half an hour off with a cup of coffee. The point is that it is impossible to know which of these interpretations is the most accurate one without more contextual material than that made available through a survey. The researcher needs at least a few glimpses into the life-worlds of the respondents in order to be able to offer an interpretation which is more than pure guesswork.

Sometimes it may be easy to identify discrepancies between statements and actions. One might, for example, conceive of the possibility that a questionnaire survey about people's media habits revealed that only a small minority of the American people regularly reads sensationalist magazines such as *The National Enquirer*; yet the circulation figures of such magazines indicate that a rather large number do read them. Very often, the task is more difficult. We humans have a selective memory – we forget, suppress and adjust our memories – and using our memory as a source, we tend to describe persons as somewhat different from the actual persons in question.

Let us assume that an anthropologist is about to study the role of ethnic identity among Aymara, one of the largest Bolivian ethnic groups, in La Paz. As always in anthropological research, several methodological approaches are possible. She might distribute 1000 questionnaires (assuming that most of the potential respondents are literate, which is unlikely), or – given time and a budget for research assistants – interview a thousand Aymara formally (with standardised questions and few alternatives). Moreover, she might approach Aymara organisations, who promote the group's interests and strive to strengthen their cultural identity and standing in society. She might also decide to zoom in on a limited number of informants, for example a neighbourhood or half a dozen extended families, and follow them around as best she could.

Which approach would be preferable? In all likelihood, a combination of the three would prove most fruitful. The questionnaire/survey would give an overview, even if superficial, that would enable her to make some initial distinctions regarding gender, age, education and other simple indicators of social belonging. The organisations would be able to show the political significance of Aymara identity in greater Bolivian society, and to indicate which changes have come about in recent history. Finally, the local networks would give her invaluable insights into the place of Aymara identity in everyday life; whether, for example, valuable resources such as jobs and favours were channelled through ethnic or supra-ethnic networks, whether class was more or less important than ethnic identity in particular situations; whether their networks extended to non-kin Aymara in other parts of the country, and so on. The fact is that all these methods have their limitations. A good anthropologist would have to supplement them with a few further approaches; she would go to public festivals and parties, she would take part in religious ceremonies, she would listen to Aymara broadcasts on the radio, and she would follow some of her informants on trips to their rural places of origin. She might not be able to do all this in the course of a single fieldwork trip, but many anthropologists return to their field sites many times in order to supplement their findings with new kinds of material. Each time she returns, briefly or for a prolonged period, she adds new layers to her understanding, meets new people and discovers new connections.

It must be added that many anthropologists are satisfied with one or two periods of fieldwork, that not all field studies last for a year or more, and that there are a lot of different ways in which an anthropological investigation can be undertaken, only a few of which have been dealt with here. Yet certain methodological requirements are definite and non-negotiable. Contextualisation is one; another consists of aiming to understand the world of the natives as far as possible in the way they themselves understand it, as a basis for further analysis.

THINGS THAT MAY GO WRONG

A lot of things can go wrong during an anthropologist's attempt at data collection. People do not behave in the same way as protons or frogs, and it is not always easy to get access to their lives. An anthropologist who virtually made his name talking about his unsuccessful fieldwork is Nigel Barley, who published, in 1983, the entertaining and commercially successful *The Innocent Anthropologist*, which was based on a fieldwork attempt among the Dowayo of Cameroon. Barley spent a long time just getting to the field, since he needed a special permit from the authorities and it quickly turned out to be nearly impossible to find a person who was willing and able to give it to him. (Many have had similar experiences, but they do not necessarily write about them.) When, at last, he arrived in the village, the local population appeared uncooperative. That is to say, they were not uninterested in him, but seemed set on having fun at his expense rather than giving him useful knowledge. The book consists of a long series of greater and lesser catastrophes, not least connected with elementary (but highly consequential) linguistic misunderstandings, and the reader is given the clear impression that Barley returned home with little to report about Dowayo culture. Many were therefore surprised to discover that in the same year as *The Innocent Anthropologist* reached the shelves, an academic monograph about the cosmology of the Dowayo was also published, penned by none other than Barley. (It must be added that Barley's humorous depiction of his fieldwork was met with strongly negative reactions in the anthropological establishment, where it was felt, among other things, that he treated his informants disrespectfully.) A conclusion may be that even unsuccessful fieldwork is rarely *entirely* unsuccessful, and it is in fact often stressed that the notorious ability of anthropologists to make fools of themselves in the field – since their knowledge about how to do and say things locally is limited – can actually be a methodological advantage. Violating norms and rules can function as a shortcut towards an understanding of the very same norms and rules.

Apart from the many true – and sometimes important – anecdotes about anthropologists' mishaps during fieldwork, the discipline also has more conventional overviews of fieldwork problems, and I shall mention the most important ones.

Ethnocentrism is a general source of distortion. It is difficult to avoid entirely, and it consists of the tendency to see other peoples from the perspective of one's own cultural categories. In its simplest form, ethnocentric research is based on an evolutionist assumption to the effect that other peoples inhabit 'lower rungs on the evolutionist ladder' than one's own, since any cultural difference can be perceived as a shortcoming.

This kind of attitude is rare in contemporary academic anthropology, but ethnocentrism does not have to be this blatantly visible in order to be effective. If, for example, one travels from egalitarian Scandinavia to Latin America, one will soon discover the inequalities between the genders; in India one will immediately discover the caste system, in Britain one will notice the entrenched class differences, and in the USA the widespread lack of personal security and social welfare. The point is not that ethnocentric bias leads the researcher to see phenomena which are not in fact 'there', but that the cultural baggage everybody, including professional anthropologists, carries with them more or less consciously, leads their attention in particular directions. One thus risks returning with a great many insights into the ways 'the x'es' represent the opposite of one's own society, although this does not necessarily give an adequate representation of *their* society. An Indian anthropologist who conducted fieldwork in a Danish village in the 1980s (Reddy 1992) was struck by the smallness of Danish families, and how little time they spent together. He was also struck by the way people seemed to treat their dogs better than their old parents.

Do these observations refer to salient characteristics of Danish community life? An anthropologist from neighbouring Sweden might instead focus on the informal life centring on the *kro* (Danish equivalent to the pub) and the comparatively relaxed attitude to alcohol. Most of the Danes who commented on Reddy's study held that he had misunderstood Danish society. This may be the case, but one cannot help asking if he had misunderstood more than the Danish researcher who returns from India and reports that the country's inhabitants are oppressed by the caste system and the demands of the family.

As soon as one is aware of the risk of ethnocentrism, it can be managed, even if it cannot be removed altogether. Above all, the education of an anthropologist entails training within a conceptual apparatus which is, at least, less ethnocentric than everyday language (even if critics have rightly pointed out that the concepts have arisen in a western context). At least, this training tempers tendencies towards ethnocentrism, since it teaches the student to raise questions framed by *anthropological* concepts instead of one's own implicit *cultural* categories. Furthermore, it is always a good idea to begin one's fieldwork by asking the local people what their main concerns are; how they see their lives, what are their main problems and so on. If one does, then one has already begun to unveil the insider's perspective.

A source of error which is complementary to ethnocentrism can be described as *homeblindness*. This problem arises, as the word implies, when fieldwork takes place in a society that the scholar has first-hand experience of. Here, the problem is not so much that the researcher misunderstands because he reads the culture through a distorted lens, but that he misses crucial dimensions because he himself takes them for granted. A fish is unlikely to discover water as long as it is surrounded by it. A general piece of advice for students planning fieldwork in their own society is therefore to allow themselves to be fished out of local waters, even if only through reading. A German anthropologist looking at the categories of German culture must be able to see them from afar – say, from a metaphoric vantage-point in the Trobriand islands – before approaching and describing them from within.

A further source of error is to do with *language*. It is a common problem that the anthropologist speaks the local language too badly (or, even if this is a smaller problem, too well – a cause of homeblindness). In the latter case, it may be a good idea to write up one's work in a foreign language (typically English, for non-native speakers), in order to achieve sufficient distance to local expressions and linguistic categories. Many either depend on working within a *lingua franca* which is not the mother-tongue of the informants (such as English, French or Portuguese in Africa, pidgin in Melanesia, or Bahasa Indonesia in Indonesia). This may render data collection cumbersome and communication less relaxed than one would wish. When one becomes aware of this problem, it can be compensated to a great extent by getting key informants who speak the *lingua franca* fluently, by giving especial attention to nonverbal communication, and by going out of one's way to find supplementary sources. A common solution is to hire an interpreter. Working through an interpreter can be necessary, but it creates its own problems. Conversations become slow and unspontaneous, and the interpreter himself may be a source of distortions. In a classic article, Gerald Berreman (1962) reveals how his interpreter in northern India made fieldwork difficult because his caste identity made it difficult for ordinary people to tell him personal details about themselves. Only after a while, after changing to another interpreter with a lower-ranking caste identity, did Berreman realise that his first interpreter had been part of the problem, not part of the solution.

The problem of language should not be exaggerated. There are anthropologists who have written excellent works about Arab societies without speaking a word of Arabic, and some of the most famous anthropological studies in existence have been carried out through interpreters or by scholars who lack anything but the most rudimentary knowledge of local languages. How well it is necessary to know the local language also depends on the topic of one's research. If one studies agricultural practices and land tenure, the demands of linguistic proficiency are likely to be less than if the topic is the local world-view.

One final problem to be mentioned, and which has more to do with academic 'ethnocentrism' than its cultural variant, is the possible tendency to believe that the life-worlds of others can be fully described and expressed verbally, through questions and answers or conversations. In fact, only a small part of the culture 'sticks out' and can be observed directly. The rest is implicit. Since academics are verbally oriented people, who are used to discussing in seminars, publishing in journals and lecturing to students, they may have an almost instinctive tendency to believe that this is also the case with others. Briefly put, there is often too much verbal data and too little observational data in all kinds of social scientific investigations, including anthropological research.

THE NATIVE POINT OF VIEW
AND THAT OF THE ANTHROPOLOGIST

It was Malinowski who wrote, in the first chapter of *Argonauts of the Western Pacific*, that the field anthropologist should strive to understand and describe the native's point of view. His contemporary and theoretical rival Radcliffe-Brown was none too impressed by this view, which seemed to imply that one just reproduced the native's chatter rather than giving a scientific account of their society. He saw the native perspective on the world as one of several kinds of raw data useful for generating explanations, but not as an end in itself. Malinowski would agree, to a certain extent, that the analysis ought to contain more than a description of local life seen from within, but the difference between the two positions was real and exists in anthropology even today. Some anthropological studies offer a wealth of detail and close-up, experience-near descriptions, while others deal with the locally seen realities more distantly, concisely or even superficially, but offer convincing explanations or clarifying overviews. In the 1930s, Radcliffe-Brown's supporters chided Malinowski's students for writing endless monographs full of painstakingly detailed accounts of even the most minor local custom or notion, without offering an explanation or a model tying the details together. They were in turn criticised for seeming to believe that the map was truer than the territory. This kind of debate is still typical of the internal dynamics of the subject (and similar debates exist elsewhere, for example in history and political science).

In the 1950s, the linguist Kenneth Pike proposed a distinction between *emic* and *etic* aspects of culture (Headland *et al.* 1990). This was derived from the distinction between phonemics and phonetics in linguistics; the significance of a given sound versus its frequency. In the context of anthropology, the (phon-) emic level refers to local cultural reality, whether it is conscious or unconscious to the people in question. The (phon-) etic level constitutes, on the contrary, the analytical language of comparison that anthropologists use to describe and make sense of the central aspects of this reality. Pike himself mentions the art of cycling as an example of emic knowledge. It is a typical 'how to' kind of knowledge; of the many who are able to ride a bike successfully, few can explain how to do it. However, they are able to demonstrate the skill for others. Similarly, people acquire a language (emically) without being able to analyse it (etically). The challenge in the anthropological translation of emic realities to etic concepts is double. On the one hand, how far can one's descriptions depart from the native's point of view before one is making things up; and, on the other hand, how close to the local reality can one pitch one's descriptions before one merely reproduces the world as locally perceived, without adding anything that might contribute to a theoretical understanding of culture and society?

Like other sciences, anthropology is bound to lead its life in the field of tension between the unique extremely rich reality it studies, and the strict ordering and simplifying tools of analysis it uses to make sense of it. There are several views on what the relationship between the emic and the etic ought to be, and indeed on the relevance of the pair of concepts itself. The most well-known proponent of the concepts in anthropology is the cultural materialist Marvin Harris. Harris argued that local people anywhere rarely or never are aware of the ultimate causes of their own actions. Their emic reality must, in other words, be trumped by the anthropologist's superior, etic explanations. One of Harris's most famous, and in its time most widely discussed, examples was his analysis of sacred cows in India (Harris 1965). According to the standard Hindu account, cows are sacred for religious reasons. According to Harris, this view constitutes an emic rationalisation of an institution which has other causes. He argues that the cows actually produce more in terms of economic value, and are more ecologically functional when deemed sacred, than they would have been if one had slaughtered and eaten them routinely. The etic explanation is, in other words, that the cows are sacred because their special status is economically and ecologically functional, although most Indians wrongly believe that religious circumstances dictate the cow's status. Harris' analysis is not accepted by most anthropologists, and one must ask why it is that similar institutions have not emerged outside of

India, if his analysis is correct. The water buffalo – a very common animal in the subcontinent – could just as well have been as sacred as the cow, given Harris' materialist, functionalist account.

In our own time, normative and political questions increasingly become relevant for research, whether researchers like it or not. In studies of immigrants in North America and western Europe, this entanglement with ethical issues is often acutely felt. When certain immigrant groups maintain cultural practices which conflict with accepted norms in the host country, how should the anthropologist-cum-specialist deal with this? The anthropologist is, in this kind of situation, both a scholar and a participant in her own society. In many western countries, debates over female circumcision, enforced marriages and hijabs (Muslim headscarves) have been debated vigorously for a number of years. In a few places, anthropologists have played an active part in these debates, and are faced with a genuine dilemma. On the one hand there are always sound *academic* reasons to view a phenomenon from the insider's perspective, relaying and interpreting the informants' perceptions and views. On the other hand, this approach often seems to conflict with *political* arguments for change. In addition, it is unclear, in a complex society, which point of view *is* the 'insider's perspective' since the populations in question are complex and represent different, often contrary positions. This situation requires a complex science able to reveal many facets and to describe their mutual interrelationship.

Since the 1970s, anthropological practices and thought have changed in several ways due to the increasing interrelatedness of nearly all parts of the world. When the discipline was fashioned in its modern form, about a century ago, large parts of the world were colonised by European imperial states. In North America, much of what was left of the native population was settled in reservations, and it would take many decades before officialdom in the USA and Canada acknowledged the rights of native Americans to self-determination, or presented official apologies for crimes committed towards them in the past. Most of the peoples anthropologists studied were illiterates settled in stateless societies (or, in the case of North America, in semi-autonomous reservations), where contact with the outside world was limited. It was unthinkable that the African or Melanesian informants should read and criticise the anthropological accounts about themselves. There was, in a word, no doubt as to where to draw the boundary between 'us' and 'them'.

In our era, the situation is strikingly different. Anthropologists could formerly write their texts in a 'timeless present tense', described by some as *the ethnographic present*, a tense sometimes giving the impression that the subjects of study remained outside of history. Contemporary anthropologists, by contrast, take great care to position their studies in a historical context of change and continuity. Anthropologists are no longer the only professional group with an interest in cultural identity and variation, and 'culture' has become a political resource exploited by large and small peoples all over the world. Former tribal peoples are now partly integrated into large-scale societies, they have their own interest groups and spokespersons, and they may not always be keen on being studied by anthropologists. Many ethnic groups worldwide feel perfectly competent to identify themselves; they have their own notions of their culture, partly influenced by anthropological concepts of culture, and they see no need for a foreign anthropologist to spend a year with them to find out who they are. The boundaries between cultures have become increasingly blurred. In addition, the subject is faced with new methodological challenges, as outlined above.

In spite of these changes, there is considerable continuity between anthropology as it was developed at the outset of the twentieth century – based on fieldwork and non-evolutionist theoretical frameworks – and contemporary practices. We still ask of our diverse world how it can be that people, born with roughly the same inborn potentials and opportunities, can turn out to be so different, and, in the next instance, what they can still be said to have in common. Still, anthropologists insist on giving priority of place to local life-worlds and on a methodological openness intended to prevent ethnocentric misjudgements. For, as Clifford Geertz has put it, if all you crave is home truths, you might as well stay at home.

FURTHER READING

Van Maanen, J. (1988) *Tales from the Field: On Writing Ethnography.* Chicago: The University of Chicago Press.
Watson, C. W. ed. (1999) *Being There: Fieldwork in Anthropology.* London: Pluto.

4
Theories

Anthropological theory may be compared to a large crossroads with busy traffic and a few, temporarily employed traffic policemen who desperately try to force the unruly traffic to follow the rules. (There are, it must be admitted, a number of minor crashes and other accidents almost every day.) Or it could be described, more harmoniously, as a coral reef, where the living corals literally build upon the achievements of their deceased predecessors.

Put differently; during the approximately 100 years that have passed since modern anthropology was established in the USA, Britain and France, many general theories have been proposed, become fashionable in and sometimes outside of anthropology, have been fiercely debated and challenged, and have disappeared, often almost without leaving visible traces. At the same time, certain insights of a methodological and theoretical nature have remained, become harder and more solid as new research has supported them, have been developed and refined under new names, and have been transmitted in modified forms to new generations. There is in fact more continuity in anthropological theory than many contemporary practitioners are willing to admit. The following pages offer some glimpses into the development of anthropological theory, and it will become clear that both perspectives – disjunction and continuity – have something to recommend them.

STRUCTURAL FUNCTIONALISM

The concepts structure and function were introduced into social science by Herbert Spencer (1820–1903), but in social anthropology they are associated especially with AR Radcliffe-Brown and his ambitious research programme, structural-functionalism. (Sociologists also have their structural-functionalism, but it is slightly different from the anthropological version and associated with theorists like Talcott Parsons and Robert Merton.)

Radcliffe-Brown and his students were particularly interested in explaining *social integration* and, more specifically, how each institution in a society contributed to the upholding of the social totality. The way they saw it, the contribution of single individuals was modest. Persons were chiefly regarded as incumbents of defined *statuses* (or roles), and the status continued to exist in unmodified form after the disappearance of the person him- or herself. Social structure was defined as the *sum of mutually defined statuses in a society*.

Even the simplest society consists of a mass of statuses. Just the relationships between members of a kin group may constitute dozens of named statuses and pairs of statuses (such as brother–sister, mother's brother–sister's son, etc.). The religious field in such a society consists of a number of further standardised social relationships, as do the political and economic fields. In practice, the structural-functionalists were especially interested in kinship when they studied traditional societies, and they assumed that kinship tended to regulate human behaviour in a number of core areas of social life, in societies with no formal educational systems, courts of law and other institutions which are state-run in modern state societies. In other words, the social structure consisted of the kinds of social relationships, abstracted from their concrete incumbents, that made up a society.

Radcliffe-Brown defined function as the contribution of an institution to the maintenance of society as a whole. He assumed that all institutions that survived in the long run, almost by definition had a function of this kind, and that dysfunctional institutions – which, in a word, contributed to the weakening of society as a whole – would eventually petrify and vanish.

A classic example of structural-functionalist thought is Radcliffe-Brown's seminal analysis of the mother's brother in South Africa (1924). In this article, he argues against evolutionist explanations and claims that the relationship had to be explained with reference to its social function. Studies of otherwise very different societies had shown that special ties often existed between the mother's brother and the sister's son; the sister's son was often allowed to 'take liberties' *vis-à-vis* his mother's brother without being punished, and in certain cases, he could inherit from him. This tie seemed to contradict the principles of the society's kinship system if it was patrilineal, which was often the case; only members of the father's kin group were then, in theory, perceived as relatives. Many scholars had explained the special status of the mother's brother by arguing that the societies in question had probably been matrilineal (or 'matriarchal', as it was sometimes erroneously described) in an earlier era, and that the special status of the mother's brother was a 'survival' from the earlier kinship system, which had later by and large been replaced with a patrilineal system.

Against this view Radcliffe-Brown claimed, with reference to South African peoples such as the Ba'thonga and the Nama, that the privileged relationship between the mother's brother and the sister's son was not due to these societies having been matrilineal in the past, but to the fact that the arrangement was socially functional. Although most resources in a patrilineal society flow through the paternal blood line, it is beneficial to give a substantial content to a person's matrilateral relationships as well. Such relationships contribute to societal stability, and Radcliffe-Brown sees them as extensions of the strong tie between mother and child. In a patrilineal society, the children belong to their father's kin group, not their mother's. Technically, they are thus not their mother's kin.

In general, the structural-functionalists were strongly against explanations derived from cultural history. Radcliffe-Brown rejected such explanations cursorily as 'conjectural history', and held that all social norms, representations and practices could be explained through their present function; they had to be functional here and now in order to be maintained. Radcliffe-Brown and his students, who included later famous anthropologists like EE Evans-Pritchard, Meyer Fortes and Max Gluckman, saw kinship, law and politics as fundamental institutions in traditional societies. The key to understanding how these societies were integrated and were being maintained (reproduced) through time, was found in these institutions. When they studied (for example) religion, they did not, therefore, limit themselves to describing how religion contributed to the maintenance of society as a whole (the function of religion), but also how it entered into political processes.

CULTURE AND PERSONALITY

The most influential American theoretical trend that developed at the same time as structural-functionalism in the interwar years had another set of aims and was based on very different assumptions about the nature of society's building-blocks. Two of Boas' students are particularly associated with this theory, namely Ruth Benedict (1887–1948) and Margaret Mead (1901–78). Benedict was regarded as the most significant theorist of the two, whereas Mead became famous for her popular monographs from Samoa and New Guinea.

The theory, or theoretical tendency, was called *culture and personality*, and entailed a narrowing of Boas' cultural relativist framework towards psychological and comparative studies. Benedict's main theoretical text, *Patterns of Culture* (1934) was a broad and ambitious attempt to show that cultures (or societies, as one would have said in Europe) had distinctive 'personality traits', which became apparent both in the shared cultural symbols and categories, and in the representations and actions of persons. Benedict distinguished between two main 'personality types', which she called, following Nietzsche, *Dionysian* and *Apollonian* cultures. The Dionysian cultures (Dionysos was the Greek god of wine) were extroverted, pleasure-seeking, passionate and often violent. The Apollonian cultures (Apollo represented order and harmony) were introverted, harmonious, puritanical, tempered and peaceful. A third pattern was labelled *paranoid*, where the inhabitants allegedly lived in constant fear and were chronically suspicious of each other.

Roughly in the same way as Radcliffe-Brown saw societies as integrated totalities, Benedict saw her cultures as consistent and seamless, and particular *Leitmotive* or patterns could be recognised in the most different contexts imaginable. Benedict differed radically from the British school in that she discussed the differences between cultural types as macropsychological differences. They could be identified in the culture as a whole, and in the individual's psyche as well. This kind of idea was alien to Radcliffe-Brown and his supporters, who were sceptical of psychological explanations. The human psyche was, in their view, itself a product of social conditions, and could thus be understood only through studying society. Malinowski, who had a lifelong interest in individual psychology, would have been more sympathetic to the American trend.

Mead was especially interested in the socialisation of children as a key to understanding cultural 'variations in personality'. It was there, and not, for example, in political institutions, that the key to understanding variation was to be found. Mead, a far more enthusiastic fieldworker than Benedict, carried out several ethnographic studies in the Pacific which aimed to show how personality is shaped, and is shaped differently, through the socialisation of children. Her first and best known book, *Coming of Age in Samoa* (1928), was simultaneously a study of socialisation in a Polynesian island and an explicit cultural critique of her own middle-class America. In Samoa, she argued, children were given love and encouragement, and they were subjected to few prohibitions. They therefore grew up to be more harmonious and happy than the cowed, disciplined and sexually frustrated American adolescents. The book is controversial and has been much discussed, but it was tremendously influential in the decades after its publication, not least outside of academia. Among other things, it was a source of inspiration for the radical youth cultures of the 1960s.

In her next book, *Growing up in New Guinea* (1930), Mead compares four Melanesian societies which display fundamental differences with respect to gender relations and the use of violence, and she discovers different patterns of culture which she in turn relates to differences in child raising. Later, she also carried out a photographic study about socialisation in Bali with her then husband Gregory Bateson (1904–80, a complex thinker whose intellectual wanderings brought him far beyond anthropology). In this study, the main conclusion was that Balinese culture 'lacked climax' in its social relationships. It was, according to Bateson and Mead, a conflict-avoiding culture where even the relationship between mother and child lacked real intimacy. In a particularly striking picture series, Bateson and Mead show a mother with an infant on her arm. The mother tries to coax the child to meet her gaze and engage actively with her, but the moment she succeeds in getting the child's attention, the mother loses interest and turns away. (It must be added that later researchers have viewed Balinese culture differently, not least after the massacres in the 1960s.)

While social anthropology in Britain was profoundly sociological in nature – the main emphasis lay, as mentioned, on politics, kinship and law, and the relationships that made up the social structure – American cultural anthropology was oriented towards both linguistics and psychology, and it has later exchanged ideas with literary studies.

AGENCY AND SOCIETY

Both Radcliffe-Brown's structural-functionalism and Benedict/ Mead's culture and personality models would prove too general, too simplistic for the anthropologists of the postwar generation. A disappointed Evans-Pritchard confessed in 1951 that structural-functionalism had failed to produce a single general 'social law' at the same level of precision as the natural sciences; and in the USA several theoretical directions emerged in the years following Boas' death, some rejecting the psychological interests of certain of Boas' students, some rejecting the philosophical idealism of the Boasian programme, and some rejecting cultural relativism as such. Others, on both sides of the Atlantic, decided instead to build on and refine aspects of one of the dominant theoretical schools, sometimes successfully.

Some of the most consequential developments in postwar Britain amounted to attempts at finding viable alternatives to structural-functionalism, whose rigid models were increasingly felt as a straitjacket even to some of Radcliffe-Brown's own students.

In 1951, the Polynesianist Raymond Firth published a book entitled *Elements of Social Organization*. It would have been an exaggeration to claim that the book led to an intellectual earthquake – Firth was far too polite – but this programmatic, theoretical book was a sign of more radical changes to come. Firth, who had been working with Malinowski for many years, was critical of the structural-functionalist faith in the ability of norms and social structure to regulate human interaction. He did not deny that such constraints existed, but he could not accept that the actions themselves were reflexes of norms and structure. His own ethnography from Tikopia suggested that people often relate rather freely to norms, and that they have to improvise and make their own decisions in order to act anyway. This is because the norms do not give sufficiently detailed instructions to anybody on how to act in a particular situation, and besides, it is not unknown for people to fail to fulfil the expectations that arise from norms. To illustrate the distinction between the abstract social structure and actual processes of interaction, Firth introduced the concept *social organisation* to describe the actual interaction taking place in a society. This he contrasted with *social structure*, which was (still) the system of interrelated statuses that made up society as an abstract template.

This distinction may seem hairsplitting, but it was more consequential than it might seem. Whereas Radcliffe-Brown regarded the individual person as a social product, Firth held that persons acted according to their own will, chose their acts and thereby were able to modify social structure. Firth's critique of structural-functionalism was, in other words, not identical to that of Evans-Pritchard. Although Evans-Pritchard now wanted social anthropology to become an interpretive science, he still felt that the objects of interpretation ought to be collective, socially shared entities. With Firth's intervention, the interest in particular individuals, so evident in Malinowski's writings, was strengthened.

Several social anthropologists rediscovered the acting individual in the 1950s. The sociologist Erving Goffman wrote pathbreaking books about role manipulation and strategic action, which were deeply influential in social anthropology, and Frederick Bailey studied strategic action in connection with caste mobility in eastern India. However, it was especially with Fredrik Barth that the new penchant for the individual became evident. Barth had studied political processes in Swat, in north-western Pakistan, for his doctoral dissertation, and in this analysis he emphasised the manipulative strategies of individuals rather than the conventional questions associated with social integration. In the programmatic paper *Models of Social Organization* (Barth 1966), he went further than possibly any other anthropologist in the direction of methodological individualism, that is the view that all societal phenomena can be studied by looking at individuals, their actions and their relations to other individuals. The opposite is methodological collectivism, which accepts the existence of collective or 'supraindividual' phenomena that cannot be studied at the level of individuals and their relationships.

Barth turned some familiar questions on their head in *Models*. Instead of presupposing that societies were integrated, he asked how social integration was at all possible, since individuals pursued their own interests which were often on a collision course with the interests of others. To him, the problem was how shared norms and values appeared at all. In order to study how interaction is gradually regulated and conventionalised in accordance with shared norms, Barth spoke about *transactions* between agents, that is strategic, calculating actions which could not be derived directly from norms and expectations, but which must be understood as driven by the desire to obtain something (value maximisation). Through repeated transactions and value negotiations, shared values and norms gradually emerged. Society was, according to this model, not given beforehand, but a dynamic, volatile 'aggregate effect' of repeated transactions. Instead of describing the interrelated statuses of society as social structure, Barth spoke about *emergent form*, that is a regularity in interaction which is seen as being continuously negotiated.

In Barth's work, the acting subject was, in other words, foregrounded. *Models* received ample attention when it appeared, and many appreciated Barth's reappraisal of the individual, a move inspired both by economic theory and by the likes of Goffman, but most colleagues agreed that he had gone too far. Individual encounters rarely arise out of nowhere, socioculturally speaking. Usually, even in transnational encounters, shared norms, rules and values exist beforehand. In one of the chapters, Barth describes a social 'point zero' which rarely occurs in ongoing social life. On the other hand, Barth's polemical text also had lasting effects, notably in making it difficult to speak about 'social structure' without problematising the concept. It is a fact that the acting individual was more commonly foregrounded in later research, and Barth's process-oriented way of thinking – the world is continuously being transformed – has also withstood the test of time. Incidentally, Barth would himself move in other directions later, and since the 1970s, his main interest has been in the study of systems of knowledge.

There was never the less something missing in Barth's elegant models of interaction, and this 'something' was exactly that which he himself had bracketed off in order to foreground the acting individual: structure. But the critique from Barth, Firth and others made it impossible to return to the old Radcliffe-Brownian concept of social structure. One was now forced to look at the interrelationship between actor and structure; between the acting individual and the constraints that limited the range of choice and gave direction to the individual. Two especially influential theories from the 1970s and 1980s, which tried to fuse a concern with individual agency with a responsible treatment of social structure, were Pierre Bourdieu's theory of practice (Bourdieu 1977) and Anthony Giddens' theory of structuration (Giddens 1984). Both have been, and remain, influential in all the social sciences, and Bourdieu's theorising has been especially important in several subfields of anthropology.

Bourdieu, who was both a sociologist and an anthropologist (with a background in philosophy) did not wish to relegate the individual to a passive role on the social stage. At the same time, however, he was interested in power and how the power differences in society distributed opportunities for choice unequally. In particular, he wanted to explore how power works through people without their noticing it. In this context, Bourdieu introduced a range of concepts intended to describe how even 'free' individuals are caught in structures they do not command and are often unaware of. Politically engaged as well as being a formidable academic, Bourdieu saw one of the tasks of social science as unveiling these structures and making them known, which in turn might make social change possible.

First, Bourdieu distinguishes between *opinion* and *doxa* when he speaks about knowledge. Doxa can be described as that which is taken for granted; that which is so self-evident (within a particular culture or discourse) that it is beyond discussion and often not even manifestly known. Opinion, in contrast, constitutes everything that is being actively discussed. If one lacks words or ideas enabling one to deny the existence of God, for example, the faith in God is doxic. If there is no questioning of the legitimacy of royalty, moreover, monarchical rule is doxic. In many societies, especially in situations of dramatic change, a mass of phenomena are moved from doxa to opinion: debate and controversy arise around matters which were formerly taken for granted. While the opposite may also happen, for understandable reasons it is less frequently noticed.

Second, Bourdieu describes embodied knowledge as *habitus* (a concept he borrowed from Mauss). This refers to the habits and skills of the body, which are both taken for granted and are hard to change. Third, Bourdieu speaks about *structuring structures*; the systems of social relations within society. People, in other words, do not choose their actions freely. They choose, but they do so within a habitus, a universe of knowledge which is partly doxic (taken for granted), and thus cannot easily be questioned, and power structures which may limit their choices severely. Free choices are therefore not illusory, but in order to understand them, it becomes important to understand causal factors that restrict them, and which, in turn, can be influenced by them.

THE STRUCTURES OF THE MIND

A rather different theoretical direction, which has exerted enormous influence over anthropological thought worldwide since the early 1950s, is structuralism. Whereas the methodological individualism of Firth, Barth and others was a reaction to structural-functionalism, structuralism appears to have more in common with it. Both Radcliffe-Brown and the founder of structuralism, Claude Lévi-Strauss, were shaped decisively by the influence of Durkheim's thought about social wholes, and the concept of structure is privileged in both. Both, moreover, had grand comparative ambitions. Lévi-Strauss tends to speak respectfully of Radcliffe-Brown, whereas he has little time for Malinowski and his tendency to reduce everything people do to some 'utility function' or other. Yet, the respective theoretical projects of Radcliffe-Brown and Lévi-Strauss are, when all is said and done, very different. Above all, they define structure in different ways. Radcliffe-Brown was chiefly concerned with demonstrating how societies were integrated, and he saw individuals as little cogs in an enormous machinery. In this regard, he had more in common with the likes of Firth and Barth than with Lévi-Strauss, since all members of the various branches of 'the British school' had their main interest in social life. Lévi-Strauss was interested in another kind of question, namely how the human mind functions; how it creates connections and orders the world in particular ways. Whereas Radcliffe-Brown's structure is a social one, Lévi-Strauss's structure is mental or cognitive; ultimately, he speaks about the structures of the brain. In a letter written to Lévi-Strauss shortly before his death in 1955, Radcliffe-Brown claimed that he would never understand the Frenchman's use of the term structure.

Lévi-Strauss's first major book was about kinship. He later wrote about systems of classification and myths, among other themes. Lévi-Strauss analysed broad cultural variations in order to achieve an understanding of the universal. The term 'binary oppositions' is often attached to structuralism, and his view is that people everywhere think through, and order the world with the help of contrasts. However, it must also be mentioned that these contrasts are in a relationship with a third, mediating instance – the amber traffic light is a classic example – and that they go through transformations (inversions, etc.) when they are transmitted between generations or peoples. A structuralist analysis of food may exemplify this: cooked food stands above raw food since culture stands above nature (the culture: nature contrast is one of Lévi-Strauss' universals). In a hierarchical society where everybody cooks their food, the symbolic significance of cooking may be turned on its head, so that the highest-ranking groups begin to eat raw or even rotten food (oysters, tartar steak, blue cheeses, cured fish, etc.). The rotten exemplifies an intermediate or third element; it stands between the raw and the cooked, and constitutes a pole in one of Lévi-Strauss's 'culinary triangles'.

The reduction of complex phenomena into simple contrasts (which may well appear as triads) or oppositions has been a main mode of analysis in structuralism since the beginning; nature: culture, man:woman, right:left, raw:cooked and so on. The third element, when it appears, can be seen as that which the simple opposition has a relationship with, which transcends the simple dichotomy. Yes and no is related to perhaps; husband and wife is related to the wife's brother, who is, in Lévi-Strauss's kinship theory, a key person.

Lévi-Strauss and others have applied structuralist method to a wide range of fields, including classification, myth, food, art and religion. His most monumental work is a four-volume study of myth, *Mythologiques* (1956–71), where he analyses different versions of a large number of Amerindian myths to show how they, through their combination of narrative and symbolic elements, and their transformations from one version to another, express certain, unchangeable properties of human thought.

Structuralism represented a synthesis of several earlier currents; the legacy from Durkheim and Mauss are obvious; it is evident, among other things, in Mauss' studies of exchange and Durkheim's totalising perspective of society and culture, in addition to their joint study of primitive classification. The influence of linguistics is just as clear; this is where the structuralist way of thinking through formal relationships was first developed in the interwar years. In addition, three further intellectual traditions ought to be mentioned in order to get a rough understanding of the place of structuralism not just in the history of anthropology, but in the history of western thought.

First, structuralism can be regarded as a kind of neo-Kantianism; a philosophical anthropology concerned with the categories of thought. Second, the influence of Jean-Jacques Rousseau is marked. Towards the end of *La pensée sauvage* (1962, Eng. tr. *The Savage Mind*, 1966), Rousseau is cited approvingly 'One needs only to look nearby if one wants to study humans; but in order to study Man, one must learn to look from afar; one must first observe differences in order to discover attributes'. Third, Lévi-Strauss is, perhaps surprisingly, a warm admirer of modern natural science, and he has a particular interest in neurophysiology. In this field, he sees the possibility that the views of structuralism on the workings of the human mind might be supported with research from a totally different field.

Structuralism, thus, is ultimately not a theory about cultural variation, but a theory about human cognitive processes. The structures that interest Lévi-Strauss are therefore far removed from cultural or social phenomena. The method he uses and advocates to achieve knowledge about these structures, however, consists of cross-cultural studies of comparable phenomena. It is only through studying the human mind in its most different manifestations, he once wrote, that we can achieve knowledge about the universally human.

Structuralism was very popular – one might even say that it was *à la mode* – from the late 1950s until around 1970, and a great number of anthropologists worldwide related actively – critically or admiringly or both – to it. It lost much of its appeal later, and has partly been replaced by a family of approaches loosely termed poststructuralist, but some structuralist ideas remain important in anthropology.

THE PRIMACY OF THE MATERIAL

The theoretical approaches presented so far in this chapter regard either the individual (sometimes perceived as a 'rational actor'), society (or social structure) or the structure of the mind as the most fundamental entity with which anthropology concerns itself. However, there exists a subset of theories which argues that studies of culture and social life need to be firmly based in studies of the material. What kind of society one lives in, how the inhabitants think and how they are ranked in relation to each other, would according to these theories, depend on material conditions. The intellectual ancestors of theorists who advocate such ideas, are Marx and Morgan rather than Durkheim and Boas. These theories can in turn be divided into two main types: those which place economics first, and those which give primacy to ecology. There are also intermediate forms, such as the theoretical trend chosen as an example below.

Until his death during the Second World War, 'Papa Franz' was the undisputed patriarch in American anthropology, and the majority of influential anthropologists in the USA were indebted to his cultural relativism and historical particularism. (An exception were the anthropologists at the University of Chicago, where Radcliffe-Brown had taught for seven years.) A small uprising was never the less under way. Several younger anthropologists wished to revitalise parts of Morgan's project which consisted of explaining cultural change through looking at technological conditions, and they expanded the perspective by including the new science of ecology in ways which Morgan could not have done. The most important representatives of this new move were Julian Steward and Leslie White. Both distinguished sharply between technological and ecological factors on the one hand, and culture (values, kinship, language, religion, etc.) on the other, and were careful not to posit a too simple causal relationship between the one and the other. Steward distinguished between the 'cultural core', which consisted of technology, ecological adaptation and property relations, and 'the rest of culture', that is religion, law, art and so on. Although the germ of change was to be found in the cultural core, the rest of culture was to a great extent autonomous and led its own life.

White's perspective was similar. He proposed a relatively simple model of cultural levels of evolution (a concept which had been used very rarely in the last 50 years of American anthropology), which he defined as the amount of available energy that was harnessed through human activity. The more energy a group or society exploited for its own ends, the higher it was placed on the evolutionary ladder. At the same time, White surprisingly regarded culture as relatively autonomous: a particular level of technological development might well be compatible with variable cultural adaptations. This was not to say that anything was possible, neither Steward nor White meant that people's perceptions, world-views or religion were determined by the material conditions, even if they constrained variation and directed change.

The main theoretical point for Steward, White and their students was that societies grew in complexity as a result of technological and economic change. Symbolic culture was bound to be influenced by these changes, although it did not follow mechanically. These anthropologists were more strongly influenced by the historical materialism of Marx than they were able to admit in the 1950s, a period when communists and socialists were not tolerated in the American public sphere.

Both ecological anthropology and different versions of Marxist anthropology never the less gained many adherents as the decade went on, and they were refined and revised in different ways; in France, leading anthropologists tried to combine Marxism with Structuralism, while some British anthropologists tried to develop Marxist analyses of kinship systems, thereby ensuring continuity with the *problematique* defined by the structural-functionalists. One of the most original and pathbreaking contributors to ecological thought was Gregory Bateson, briefly mentioned above as a husband and collaborator of Margaret Mead. Bateson was no ecological or materialist determinist, but he applied an ecological *way of thinking* to a wide range of phenomena. He was one of the founders of cybernetics (the theory of self-regulating systems), and he also had a background in biology (his father was the famous geneticist William Bateson, and named his son after Gregor Mendel). In Bateson's view, all systems had some properties in common. For example, the elements in dynamic systems react through feedback and to feedback from other elements in the system. The loops of feedback and negative feedback (the lack of feedback) create repercussions everywhere in the system, and the ensuing process of reproduction and self-transformation never ends. Unlike for example White, Bateson did not believe in the primacy of material factors. On the contrary, it was only when they entered into a dynamic relationship to 'another something' and created differences that made a difference, that they were worthy of attention, and it might just as well be ideas as things that started processes of systemic change.

INTERPRETATION RATHER THAN EXPLANATION

Among the theoretical perspectives of enduring significance that were launched in the second half of the twentieth century, interpretive anthropology is most squarely placed in the Boasian tradition. This, in spite of the fact that the leading spokesman for this trend, Clifford Geertz, was just as deeply influenced by European sociology and social philosophy as by the parental generation in American cultural anthropology.

Interpretation is far from a novelty in anthropology, and there are good reasons to claim that all good anthropological research has a crucial element of interpretation, whether recognised by the researcher or not. Ethnographic fieldwork itself is an interpretive activity; it is impossible to observe the world directly without a *pre-understanding* that creates a frame of interpretation for whatever it is that one sees and hears. That which a trained observer of social life records, must necessarily be interpreted and incorporated into an overarching narrative or account. As mentioned already, Malinowski spoke in 1922 about the significance of seeing the world from *the native's point of view*, and in the last decades of his career, Evans-Pritchard regarded social anthropology as an interpretive discipline rather than a science with pretensions akin to those of the natural sciences.

Yet Geertz and other interpretive American anthropologists did bring something new into the subject. If we restrict ourselves to Geertz himself, who is the world's most widely quoted anthropologist both inside and outside of the discipline, it is hopefully not too disrespectful to state that roughly half of his contribution has consisted of describing, in flowing, beautiful prose, aspects of anthropology that have been part of the discipline's tacit knowledge since the advent of long-term fieldwork. This is arguably the case with his famous essay 'Thick Description' (1983). The main point here is that a good ethnographic account must include a lot of contextual description for the ethnographic data to be understandable. A simple example, which he borrows from the philosopher Gilbert Ryle, is blinking. In a certain sense, blinking may be described as a mechanical movement of the eyelids, but such a description tells us nothing about what blinking *means*. Its significance depends on the context in which it occurs, and the meaning of blinking naturally varies cross-culturally.

Most anthropologists follow Geertz up to this point without raising an eyebrow. We may never the less distinguish between a weak and a strong hermeneutic (interpretive) programme. A weak hermeneutic programme, which most would subscribe to, accepts the importance of interpretation in data collecting and ethnographic description; while a strong hermeneutic programme, as launched by Geertz, claims that the entire analysis must be interpretive. In fact, Geertz has argued that cultures may be 'read' as if they were texts, and has gone far, especially early in his career, towards trying to show that cultures are integrated in a 'logico-meaningful' way. As in literature studies, the reading of a culture entails the continuous relating of details to the totality and *vice versa*; the part is only meaningful in relation to the whole and the whole in relation to the parts. Moreover, Geertz holds that most members of a culture have roughly the same world-view, the same values and so on; and he insists that a culture is integrated *from within*, that is through native concepts and meaningful categories. This implies that the task of research primarily consists of penetrating, understanding and describing culture systematically the way it is experienced locally; not to explain it by recourse to 'etic' terms of comparison or explanation, be they structuralist, materialist or otherwise. Finally, Geertz emphsises that culture is expressed through *shared, public symbols*, that is meaningful communication. It is thus unnecessary to guess what lurks inside the heads of informants to understand their culture; it is sufficient to study the ongoing communication that takes place between them.

Like other influential theorists, Geertz has been criticised from many quarters, and the main objections are these: cultures are in fact not particularly tightly integrated, their boundaries are fuzzy, and there is a great deal of individual and group-based variation within any culture. It has moreover been pointed out that Geertzian hermeneutics inadvertently creates a harmonious model of society where exploitation and power discrepancies are neglected. Finally, many feel that anthropology should have somewhat larger ambitions than making sense of local universes of meaning; it should also explain how they arise, and it should engage in systematic, scientific comparison in order to achieve more general and theoretically sophisticated understandings of social and cultural dynamics than a purely interpretive anthropology is able to generate.

ANTHROPOLOGICAL THEORY TODAY

Contemporary anthropological theory appears a bit like the crossroads described at the beginning of this chapter, and for outsiders or new students, it may seem bewildering and surprising that scholars who are concerned with similar questions and use some of the same methods in describing them, speak such different theoretical languages. However, as this overview of some main trends and twentieth-century developments indicates, there is both continuity and change in the development of anthropological theory. The changes in theoretical perspectives have happened fast compared to other sciences. Some believe that this is because anthropology is a 'young science', but in my view, the ongoing revision and replacement of models of explanation and interpretation are caused by some intrinsic properties of the discipline itself. First, the raw material of anthropology – people, societies, cultures – is constituted differently from that of the natural and quantitative sciences, and it can be formalised only with great difficulty and at the peril of losing significant aspects. Second, there has been a tremendous development in terms of growth in high-quality empirical material over the last century, and since anthropological theory is deeply tied to observation, it must necessarily change when masses of new data are put on the table. In the second part of this book, numerous examples will be called upon to illustrate how this happens.

Since the mid-1980s, *eclecticism* has been a common theoretical strategy, that is combinations of elements derived from diverse sources. There has also been a tendency towards increased modesty concerning the explanatory power of anthropology. The grand theories which aimed to explain everything from the historical growth of culture to the universal mechanics of society, have been dismissed by most practitioners. Besides, there has been a marked tendency towards increasingly critical self-examination within anthropology, not least because of mounting criticism from some of the research subjects themselves. Many of them now prefer to describe themselves, rather than have foreign 'experts' do it in ways they often perceive as demeaning and distorting.

The presentation of theoretical perspectives above has indicated that there is a tight connection between the questions a scholar tries to find answers to, and the perspective he or she applies to the world. It may be said that there are three large families (or kin groups) of fundamental questions that have been raised again and again by anthropologists. The first group of questions are: what is it that makes people do whatever they do? This kind of research question will generate analytic models that take their point of departure in individuals and relationships between individuals. Sometimes psychological mechanisms will be drawn in, and occasionally, the analyst will add a supplementary macroperspective to his or her micromaterial; that is a description of external factors (economic circumstances, the state, etc.) that create and constrain the space for activity and contribute to explaining change.

The second group of questions are: how are societies or cultures integrated? This kind of question requires another kind of empirical material, and will to a greater extent look at institutions and shared patterns of significance rather than individuals. The individuals become exemplars rather than independent units of analysis.

Third: to what extent does thought vary from society to society, and how much is similar across cultures? When this question is dealt with, the method will necessarily concentrate on systems of knowledge and their internal properties.

Actual research projects are naturally much more precisely formulated. For one thing, particular issues are associated with certain regions (peasant societies in Latin America, witchcraft in southern Africa, gender in Melanesia); and for another, there are many specialisations in anthropology (from medical anthropology to the anthropology of ethnicity) with their own agendas and concepts. Yet these, I maintain, are the main *fundamental* questions raised in the discipline.

As already shown, there are important differences between the kinds of answers given to each of the questions mentioned. Cultural materialists offer different answers to structural-functionalists concerning how societies are integrated, and a structuralist and a hermeneuticist would offer very different accounts about how thought and knowledge are organised in different societies. The theory gives a framework, a direction and not least an indication of where to look when doing fieldwork. When there is theoretical disagreement, there may be several reasons for this; there may be disagreement as to which questions are the most relevant ones, about which kind of data is the most telling, and – not least – there may be disagreement about how to interpret the empirical material.

Wandering about in the maze of theoretical orientations, some may ask if theory is at all necessary. Does not the job ultimately consist in collecting empirical material and making sense of it, and does one need theory to accomplish such a task? The answer to the final part of the question is yes. There is an unlimited potential number of facts in the world, and we need criteria to judge some of them as more significant than others. Moreover, we need criteria enabling us to order the empirical material in a particular way. Finally, we need criteria for evaluating the ultimate significance of the empirical material; does it say something about human nature, perhaps, or about power in traditional societies, or about reciprocity as a basic quality of human relationships? All published work in anthropology has an element of theory, even if it is not always explicit. The selection of issues and empirical material entails a theoretically based narrowing of the world. At the same time, anthropology carries with it an important *inductive bias*; theory should ideally not be enforced upon the observations, but should grow out of them. If theory and empirical material do not fit together at all, it is not the latter's fault.

The Oxford anthropologist Godfrey Lienhardt once wrote that a good anthropological monograph contained an elephant of data and a rabbit of theory, but the stew must be cooked in such a way that the taste of the rabbit was felt in every spoonful. Although it raises spectacularly abstract questions sometimes, anthropology is not a subject for abstract speculation. It can be a kind of empirical philosophy; anthropologists raise some of the same questions as philosophers, but discuss them – after having learned theoretical thinking from philosophers – by making them engage with social and cultural facts. Social anthropology can be a kind of microsociology, which studies power and social relations from below. Significant parts of the discipline are located near the frontier with other disciplines. The relationship between many American anthropologists and literary studies has been close in later years, thanks to some of Geertz's heirs and critics, whose analyses are highly sensitive to questions of style and metaphor. The relationship to ecology is also close in some quarters, where the research questions concern humanity and nature. Economics and psychology also have their productive frontierlands bordering on anthropology, and the kinship with history has become increasingly evident since Evans-Pritchard pronounced that social anthropology was more like history than like the natural sciences.

Thematically speaking, anthropology is so broad that it moves, almost chronically, in the frontier areas, at the same time as it nearly always retains its own identity. The shared identity that keeps the discipline together in spite of sometimes strikingly divergent research agendas, can be summed up as an insistence on regarding social and cultural life from within, a field method largely based on interpretation, and a belief (albeit variable) in comparison as a source of theoretical understanding. Most social and cultural anthropologists (but not all) regard evolutionist theories of cultural change as irrelevant or wrong; and most (but again not all) reject neo-Darwinist theories which attempt to account for social and cultural life as the products of our evolutionary history.

In the second part of this book, it will become evident that contemporary theoretical perspectives often combine influence from the classic theories in ways which create a greater complexity than that which was formerly common. In this way, unfortunate dualistic figures of thought are avoided, at the expense of losing simple, elegant explanations. For example, no self-respecting contemporary anthropologist would propose a distinction between 'modern' and 'traditional' societies as anything but a provisional analytic tool, to be discarded the moment one dips into the substance of social reality. We know too much about the problems associated with these concepts, the 'mixtures' typical of nearly every society in existence, and the variations within each category, for such a distinction to be defensible. Besides, the contradiction between individualist and collectivist (or actor-based versus system-based) accounts, seen as a conflict in the 1960s and 1970s, is largely gone. In its stead, models trying to grasp both the acting individuals and the systemic properties constraining them are taken for granted by most contemporary anthropologists.

What characterises anthropological research today more than anything, is the recognition of complexity; the world is complex, cultures are complex, communities are complex, and analytical strategies must acknowledge complexity. In spite of this, I intend to indulge in a few attempts at ordering and simplification in the following chapters, just as I have done in the first half of this book, and will present some of the key fields in anthropological research. A caveat is necessary. It would be misleading, bordering on being disingenuous, to claim that these are *the* central themes, or to insinuate that research 'has now come so far' that it has reached watertight solutions to the problems they raise. But if social and cultural anthropology can be seen as a multistorey building with half a dozen flats on each level, I am prepared to defend the view that the chapters that follow properly belong to the two bottom floors.

FURTHER READING

Moore, Henrietta, ed. (1999) *Anthropological Theory Today*. Cambridge: Polity.

Moore, Jerry (1997) *Visions of Culture: An Introduction to Anthropological Theories and Theorists*. Walnut Creek: AltaMira Press.

Part 2
Fields

5
Reciprocity

In everyday language, the word reciprocal usually refers to a relationship in which two groups or persons give the same things to each other. In anthropology, the concept of reciprocity has a different and more specific meaning. It refers to exchange in a wide sense. This kind of activity has had a central place in anthropology for generations, at least since the publication of Marcel Mauss' *The Gift* (*Essai sur le don*, 1925). Mauss's erudite and wide-ranging essay about the gift is an untypical text in anthropology, at least seen from an Anglo-American viewpoint, and reminds us that French anthropology has followed its own itinerary. Mauss did not himself carry out any fieldwork, and yet he is considered just as important as the foremost of his contemporaries in Britain and the USA. *The Gift* shows why. Mauss was familiar with many languages and knew not only virtually the entire ethnographic literature, but was also widely read in sociology and cultural history. *The Gift*, incidentally, contains more cultural history than contemporary ethnography, and it begins with a quotation from the Norse epic *Håvamål* about the importance of hospitality. Mauss then moves on to discussing gift-giving in a number of 'archaic societies', taking sideways glances to contemporary anthropology and ending with a conclusion where he candidly discusses current social problems in French society against the background of his earlier analysis.

Mauss makes a threefold distinction in his account of cultural history. First, he describes societies where gift-giving is universal and fundamental for social integration. The main sources for this kind of society are historical. Second, there is an intermediate category, where social institutions – the state, trade and so on – have taken over some of the original functions of the gift. Third and finally, he describes the modern, market-oriented societies where gift exchange, according to Mauss, has been relegated to a more marginal role.

The gift contains three elements: the obligation to give, the obligation to receive and the obligation to return the gift. Gift exchange is in theory voluntary, but in practice obligatory. When a person offers a gift or *préstation* (which can be either material or immaterial), the receiver is obliged to offer something in return, usually after a certain lapse of time. In western society, Christmas gifts are often mentioned as remnants of the original tradition of gift exchange, but it is easy to see that Mauss' principles are also valid in many other areas. If someone invites you to a dinner party, you are expected to invite them in return when you have your own party. In Britain, millions of inhabitants keep alive an old tradition of reciprocity through buying rounds at the pub. Among friends and families in society, it is considered an insult to offer to pay for favours. Practices such as the circulation of second-hand children's clothing among relatives and friends, and voluntary community work, are also common in many contemporary western societies, and contribute considerably to creating strong mutual obligations and social cohesion locally.

In those societies where gift exchange is the very foundation of social integration, in the absence of formal political institutions, 'debts of gratitude' (as we might say) establish ties between most of the adult inhabitants. Everybody finds him- or herself in a maze of vague commitments and obligations to others, which in certain cases may include, in one way or another, most of the other villagers. Even in 'foreign policy', gift exchange may be the most important activity, and again it is easy to see that the logic of this institution has survived in contemporary state societies; we are reminded of it every time the newspapers report that a politician has received a lavish, morally problematic gift during a state visit, a gift which might compromise his political integrity.

Mauss devoted special attention to two contemporary ethnographic studies. The first is the investigation undertaken by Boas and his collaborators concerning the enigmatic *potlatch* institution on the north-western coast of North America. The second is Malinowski's study of the *kula* ring in Melanesia, which had just been published when Mauss wrote his essay.

Both these institutions require an explanation. Neither is a simple exchange system where the meaning and social significance of the exchange are easy to understand. To begin with the *kula* trade: The *Kula* is a regional exchange system which encompasses many of the islands in Melanesia, and where the commodities which circulate – beautiful shells and necklaces made of dolphin teeth – do not seem to have an obvious economic value. Moreover, nobody is allowed to keep them for good either. The recipient of a *kula* object is obliged to send it onwards after a period.

The *Kula* takes place between people living in island and coast communities, and Kiriwina (the Trobriand island where Malinowski did his fieldwork) forms part of the circle. The different kinds of valuables circulate in opposite directions (clockwise vs. anti-clockwise). It is economically demanding to equip and prepare a *Kula* expedition; it is time-consuming and risky, and the crew needs to bring both food and gifts other than the *kula* objects themselves. The people involved have a decentralised economy based on horticulture and fishing, and only the most powerful men can afford to equip *kula* expeditions. It has been suggested that goods with 'real economic value' might circulate along with the symbolic goods in focus, but this hypothesis was rejected on empirical grounds. Yet, participation in the *kula* trade can doubtless strengthen a man's political standing.

Mauss mentions that similar, intricate and wide-ranging systems of exchange of symbolic goods exist in other parts of the Pacific as well (a fact Malinowski does not take note of), and argues that the system leads to a regional integration which creates peace, and which may create channels for the exchange of other values as well, tangibles as well as intangibles. Malinowski's own explanation has also stood the test of time rather well. He admits that the institution has inexplicable elements, but at the same time strongly emphasises *personal fame* as a motivating factor. Every *kula* object is accompanied by the names of everybody who has had it in his possession, and when it is transferred to a new holder, the entire list of names must be recited. In other words, one becomes a 'man of renown' over a large area by being involved in the *kula* trade. This view was supported, but also modified, in Annette Weiner's re-study of the Trobrianders (Weiner 1976).

Both Mauss' and Malinowski's analyses of the *kula* trade show that exchange does not need to be 'economically profitable' in order to function efficiently, and besides, they indicate that economics need to be framed by cultural accounts. What it is that is in demand, which kinds of valuables are bought and sold, and which objects or immaterial values cannot be transferred freely; all this varies cross-culturally. If we want to understand why it may be morally unproblematic in our society to sell plumbing, but morally dubious to sell sex, or why it is that a house in a prestigious location may cost four times as much as an identical house in a less desirable area, we need an understanding of values and exchange systems which goes far beyond the merely economic. In fact, there is no such thing as anything 'purely economic' in economic anthropology. All economies have a local, moral, cultural element.

Mauss's second contemporary (or near-contemporary) example, to which he devoted more space than the *kula* ring, was the spectacular *potlatch* institution among peoples like the Tlingit and the Haida on the north-west coast of North America. By the time of Boas' research, the custom had nearly died out, but it was well documented in numerous sources, written as well as oral. Traditionally, the chiefs of these groups had organised lavish feasts to which they invited each other plus an ample entourage. The purpose of these feasts seems to have been to surpass one another in *conspicuous consumption* (to use the sociologist Thorstein Veblen's concept). Apart from the food, the drink and the costly gifts given to the visitors, large amounts of goods were simply thrown into the ocean or burned. Woven carpets, fish, copper plates – in the old days, even slaves are said to have been thrown into the ocean – were destroyed as evidence of the incredible wealth and power of the hosting chief. The *potlatch* institution was subjected to the usual (in Mauss' view universal) rules of reciprocity, but when it was the neighbour's turn, he was obliged to try to surpass the previous host in extravagance. *Potlatch* can be described (and is described by Mauss) as a perverted form of reciprocity, where the goal is to show off rather than establish bonds of mutual commitment. It would incidentally not be difficult to find *potlatch*-like phenomena in contemporary western society if one cares to look.

It may be objected that Mauss exaggerates the difference between his three main kinds of society. Reciprocity has been shown to be more important in modern societies than he seemed to be aware of. When he looked at France in the 1920s, he saw primarily a society where morally based social relations had been replaced by sterile and unemotional market forces; where the worker was tied to the manager only through a formal, contractual relationship, and where the family had been reduced to an auxiliary institution for the system of reproduction. At this time, social scientists commonly viewed industrial society as alienating and demeaning, and in this regard, Mauss differed little from his uncle Durkheim. However, later studies have shown that social relationships based on reciprocity remain very central in contemporary industrial societies, not least in informal social life, and nothing suggests that this is about to change. In Mauss' classification there is not only an implicit romanticisation of traditional societies, but also an implicit evolutionism – societies develop from reciprocity to market economies – which has been shown to be simplistic.

Although this point seems to contradict Mauss' analysis, it confirms his theory at a deeper level; reciprocity has now been shown to be a fundamental aspect of sociality, and a social system lacking the moral commitment attached to the exchange of gifts in a wide sense (including favours/services) is difficult to imagine.

FORMS OF INTEGRATION

A theory which had much in common with that of Mauss, was developed a couple of decades after *The Gift*. With the publication of *The Great Transformation* (1944), Karl Polanyi, an economic historian, presented a theory which held that societies could be economically integrated according to three distinct principles.

First, they could function according to the principle of *reciprocity*, that is barter or direct exchange of goods and services, based either on trust or on immediate return payment. Second, they could function according to the principle of *redistribution*. Those who produced anything deemed valuable had to give a certain proportion of it to a recognised authority, who then redistributed the surplus among the inhabitants. Taxes are the most familiar form of payment with a view to redistribution in our society, and similar practices are more common in traditional societies than many people are aware of. Third, societies might be integrated according to the *market principle*, where both goods and labour were bought and sold in an anonymous market (i.e. buyer and seller did not have to know each other), which would integrate a potentially enormous number of persons into a shared social system.

Polanyi's book exerted enormous influence on the burgeoning field of economic anthropology, and he, not an anthropologist himself, drew widely on anthropological studies of 'primitive economics'. It must be noted that the book is largely an account of western economic history – the great transformation alluded to in the title is the transition to a capitalist economy – and that his deepest preoccupation amounts to a critique of liberal market economies. In his view, reciprocity and redistribution are just as natural, and more humane, forms of economic interaction than the raw, competitive market. (As readers will have discovered by now, the main ideological thrust of Polanyi's book retains its contemporary relevance today, 60 years on.)

In an appendix to his chapter about traditional economic systems, Polanyi makes some observations which are directly relevant to economic anthropology. He argues that maximisation is not 'natural' for humankind. In most known cases, economic activity is a matter of survival, as well as a means to establish contacts with others through reciprocity. He who does not follow the rules is excluded from crucial social networks, and the price is usually too high to pay. Polanyi also points out that economic systems form part of social totalities, and are accordingly governed by the same moral norms that are valid in other contexts. Moreover, he rejects the common view which holds that humans 'in a state of nature' were self-sufficient at the household level, and refers to Firth's Polynesian research, which indicates that even people with simple technologies and a modest ability to produce surpluses are involved in wide-ranging exchange activities. Finally, Polanyi argues that reciprocity and redistribution have not only been the governing principles of integration in small and simple societies, but that they have also functioned rather well in large and powerful empires.

Although it was fashioned in another intellectual context, namely that of a radical critique of capitalism, Polanyi's critical history about the growth of liberal economics was compatible with, and a major source of inspiration for, the field of economic anthropology. Polanyi had criticised a simple evolutionist idea according to which market economies are the end product of a long developmental process; he had rejected the notion, common among economists, that humans primarily strive to maximise utility (even if it happens at the expense of others), and he had demonstrated that the economic life of humans varied significantly. Most importantly, he refused to view economics in isolation from the totality of social life.

Although he does not cite Mauss, there are many commonalities between the latter's account of gift exchange and Polanyi's analysis of the growth of liberalism. Both regard psychological motivations as being complex, where personal gain, consideration for others and the need to be socially acceptable play a part. Both regard reciprocity as the strongest 'glue' at our disposal for keeping societies together, and both were politically radical without being Marxists.

AGAINST MAXIMISATION

Among the many anthropologists who have been inspired by both Mauss and Polanyi, the most influential has arguably been Marshall Sahlins. His important collection of essays *Stone Age Economics* (1972) is largely devoted to forms of reciprocity in traditional societies. There, he draws upon, discusses and refines insights from, among others, Mauss, Polanyi and the Russian peasant researcher Chayanov.

Sahlins distinguishes between three forms of reciprocity. The first, the least interesting here, is called *balanced reciprocity*, that is market trade, tit-for-tat exchange. Neither Polanyi nor Mauss held, incidentally, that buying and selling were absent from traditional societies, but the markets were 'peripheral', i.e. society would have chugged on without them. The second form of reciprocity described by Sahlins, *generalised reciprocity*, is reminiscent of Mauss' concept of the gift. In this realm, there is no acknowledged pricing mechanism and no explicit demands for return gifts, but every person involved knows the rules intuitively. The third form of exchange discussed by Sahlins serves to remind the reader that where there are moral communities, there are also boundaries. There scarcely exists a single society which does not distinguish between 'us' and 'them'. He uses the term *negative reciprocity* about all forms of economic deception, where one tries to reap the benefit without paying the cost. Fraud, theft and even ruthless haggling are included in this category.

Using a simple, elegant model, Sahlins indicates where the boundaries are drawn between the three forms of reciprocity in an ideal-typical traditional society. Generalised reciprocity is the norm within the household and among relatives. Balanced reciprocity applies in the vicinity, usually the village or cluster of villages with a shared identity, whereas negative reciprocity is accepted in dealings with strangers. Sahlins may easily be criticised for not elaborating his model by referring to a variety of societies where the principles are articulated in different ways; most of the examples he draws upon are from the Pacific region. The model is never the less good as an ideal type and a starting point for analysis, because it offers an accurate, parsimonious set of concepts tailored to investigate the moral content of different exchange relations and to show how morality, economics and social integration are interwoven. Just where the boundary should be drawn between generalised, balanced and negative reciprocity is an empirical question; the point is that the three forms say something about the quality of social relations, which in turn can say something about society as a whole and its boundaries *vis-à-vis* outsiders.

In his discussion of Chayanov, Sahlins develops a similar argument. 'Chayanov's rule', based on studies of pre-revolution Russian peasant societies, states that in a peasant household, which by definition is only partly integrated into the market economy (one produces food for one's own needs in addition to buying and selling in the market), the labour input of each household member depends on which proportion of the household members are economically active. If, for example, four out of six household members work in the fields, each of them is likely to work less than what would have been the case if only three out of six had been economically active. Sahlins generalises this principle, deriving from Chayanov's own research, to all peasant societies, and he uses it as an argument against the view that it is somehow part of human nature to 'maximise utility'. Many of the households would evidently have been able to produce a larger economic surplus, had everybody worked harder, but they had other priorities.

Other scholars have in a certain sense turned Mauss on his head, and have pointed out how 'generalised reciprocity' or the logic of gift exchange creates bonds of dependence which may often be described as semi-feudal, and which may be economically inefficient (Mauss was aware of this latter point). Pierre Bourdieu has argued along these lines in several of his writings about symbolic power, for instance in an example where a North African mason, who has spent some years in France, insists on receiving money instead of taking part in a ritual meal with the contracting party. The mason rejects, in Bourdieu's (1990) words, 'the formula according to which the symbolic alchemy aims at transforming the labour and its value to kind gifts'. In this kind of argument, we may also recognise the resistance against the logic of the gift found in the labour movement.

It must be stressed that the influence of *The Gift* far surpasses the limited field of economic anthropology. In his book about the elementary structures of kinship, to be discussed in the next chapter, Lévi-Strauss shows his indebtedness to Mauss. The exchange of women, the very 'super-gift' in traditional societies, is the fundamental building-block in Lévi-Strauss's model, and he got the idea from Mauss. Lévi-Strauss has also pointed out that Mauss, as early as 1925, defined the social world as 'a world of symbolic relationships' and thereby encouraged a science which connected the mental life of the individual to the collective life of the group. Even more important for Lévi-Strauss was Mauss' general intention, evident in many of the latter's scattered essays, to identify hidden patterns and regularities in an empirical reality which might seem infinitely complex. For the systems of exchange to function in the long term, Lévi-Strauss argues, they must be regularised to such an extent that they may be described formally. Groups and persons are related to each other according to an invisible key which ensures that their mutual relationships are regulated and constant.

It was the combination of Mauss's thought about reciprocity between individuals and groups, and structural linguistics, that gave the impetus to Lévi-Strauss' own theory. Faithful to the logic of the gift, Lévi-Strauss offered a return gift which was just as lavish as his mentor's, namely the most spectacular theoretical edifice of the last century, structuralism.

THE INALIENABLE

As suggested, the principle of reciprocity has proved to be illuminating far beyond the research field usually described as economic anthropology. Sahlins honed the conceptual apparatus

and attuned it to contemporary concerns; Bourdieu inverted
the model, showing how apparent generosity might conceal
misuse of power; and Lévi-Strauss extended and transformed
reciprocity thinking to encompass the exchange of women and
the ensuing establishment of affinality (in-law relations). But we
are still not finished with Mauss and the concept of reciprocity.
A continuous trickle of anthropological publications, many of
them very sophisticated and influential, show the continued
impact of *The Gift*. One of the most inspiring recent studies is
Annette Weiner's *Inalienable Possessions* (1992). Unlike Mauss and
most of his successors, Weiner does not look at the exchange
of gifts and services, but at the flip side, one might say logical
implication, of the institution; in every social community, the
line is drawn somewhere; there are possessions which simply
cannot be exchanged or given away as gifts. They constitute her
'inalienable possessions'.

Mauss was aware that certain objects and knowledge were secret,
sacred or private and could not be given away or exchanged. In
his discussion of the *potlatch*, he refers to 'certain copper plates'
which are displayed, but which cannot be imparted. Where there
is reciprocity and trade, there is also something which cannot
be transferred, bartered, sold or otherwise shared with others,
be it things, knowledge or actions. In a discussion about Weiner
and Mauss, Maurice Godelier (1999) writes that 'these things
which are kept – valuables, talismans, knowledges, rites – confirm
deep-seated *identities and their continuity through time'*. Weiner
is, in other words, especially interested in understanding why
certain things flow between individuals and families, and why it is
that certain things (including immaterials) cannot be transferred
freely. The key to an understanding of these restrictions may
be found in a term Mauss uses himself, namely the Polynesian
word *hau*. The *hau* of an object is its spiritual innermost being,
its soul as it were, which makes it necessary to treat it, and its
receiver or giver, with respect, and which ties it to its place of
origin forever. *Hau* transcends the mere materiality of an object,
the mere instrumentality of a service.

The learned debate, especially engaging scholars of the Pacific
and Melanesia, propelled by Mauss' pathbreaking study may at
a first glance seem esoteric. Yet there are intriguing similarities
between the societies discussed by Weiner and Godelier, and

modern western ones. There are definite rules, albeit implicit, which regulate reciprocity and set boundaries between its forms in our societies as well. At children's birthday parties, there are finely attuned rules which define which gifts are appropriate; they should be neither too expensive nor too cheap, and they should belong to certain categories of objects, not others. A typical short-term return gift at adult dinner parties in the same kind of society is a bottle of wine or a flower bouquet; but one cannot credibly bring along say, a toaster for the host(-ess). A typical long-term return gift would be a similar dinner party, not a trip to Italy.

What, then, are the 'inalienable possessions' in western societies? It is common to assume that 'anything' can be bought and sold in a 'fully developed market economy', unlike in traditional societies where sacred objects, ritual incantations, magical formulas and indeed – in many cases – land and labour are inalienable. Yet there are clear restrictions in western societies as well. Sale and purchase of sex is considered immoral, and in this regard, western societies have established a clearer boundary between different forms of reciprocity than would be the case in many traditional societies, where there are areas of ambiguity between what we would call love relationships and prostitution. In western societies, it is not morally unproblematic to sell a family farm one has inherited; and under most circumstances, it is morally dubious to give away the horrible trinkets one inherited from an aunt or received for one's wedding. These are just a few random examples. In many social environments, moreover, there exist forms of secret knowledge and secret rites, which express the identity of the community, and which must not be known to outsiders. The most obvious examples are the rites and incantations of secret or semi-secret societies such as freemasons; but similar 'inalienable possessions' exist in other social environments as well. The esoteric language of certain academics has clear similarities with the secret knowledge of traditional cults. It has even been suggested, in an article by Simon Harrison (1999), that *identity* could be seen as an inalienable possession; that a group's innermost *hau*, which defines who its members are, can be unnegotiable. To some, this is stretching Mauss too far; to others, it shows the universality of his thought.

CONSUMPTION

The reciprocity principle continues to be used in economical anthropology, although it is more narrowly defined. In a series of studies from the 1950s, rather more influenced by Polanyi than by Mauss, Laura and Paul Bohannan showed how the economy of the Tiv in central Nigeria was being transformed by the modern (colonial) market principle. Like many traditional peoples, the Tiv distinguished between several 'economic spheres' before colonialism, where different kinds of objects circulated separately. They had a subsistence sphere, where foodstuffs and certain handicrafts were sold and bought according to the principle of balanced reciprocity; there was a sphere reserved for especially valuable goods (a certain white cloth and brass rods), and there was a separate sphere for the exchange of women between kin groups. The Bohannans showed that there existed among the Tiv strict rules regarding *conversion* between the spheres, so that one could not 'buy' a woman no matter how many chickens one had to offer. When general-purpose money was introduced in colonial times, the distinction between the spheres collapsed, since money became 'the measuring stick of all things'. In this way, the Bohannans argued, an important moral dimension of the economy collapsed, since everything became comparable with everything else and anything could be purchased with money. The status of women appears to have declined.

In later years, many anthropologists have carried out research on consumption in modern societies. In this area, Mauss' and Polanyi's early studies are both built upon and transcended. Both saw the modern market economy as deeply amoral, since enduring personal relationships were not created through the ongoing economic intercourse. If I buy a bus ticket, a packet of cigarettes or even a second-hand car from someone, the transaction is completed the moment I pay up, and theoretically I may never see the salesman again. (Regarding the last example, written laws instead of personal obligations ensure that the rules are followed.) In an original study from Båtsfjord in Finnmark, northern Norway, Marianne Lien (1992) showed that economic spheres may coexist even in modern monetary economies. In her example, self-caught fish and self-picked cloudberries do not enter the market; they can be given away, but they cannot be sold. Another anthropologist,

Runar Døving (2001), has similarly shown, in a study based on fieldwork in south eastern Norway, that it may be extraordinarily impolite to ask for 'just a glass of water' when one is visiting. In his example, the hosts do everything they can to make the guest accept beer, a soft drink, coffee, tea, even herbal tea, to avoid the horror of having her sit there drinking tap water. As Mauss could have commented; refusing to receive a gift may be the ultimate offence. It is tantamount to refusing sociality.

An ambitious analysis of consumption, deeply influenced by Mauss, is Daniel Miller's *A Theory of Shopping* (1998). Miller carried out fieldwork on a high street in north London, among women on shopping rounds, and reaches some surprising conclusions. Above all, he claims that shopping is far from being an unsocial, selfish kind of activity, but reflects and strengthens intimate social relationships. The women very often shop for items intended for family members and close friends. Moreover, whenever they buy something for themselves, they do so with the views of others in mind.

Miller sees shopping as an expression of reciprocity, but he also compares it with *sacrifice*. Seen from outside, sacrifice appears to be a kind of ritual which is intended to confirm the sacrificers' belief in a divinity because the act of sacrifice brings them into contact with something supernatural. Miller concludes that shopping is concerned with exactly the same objective. One buys things for others, not because one desires them, but because one wishes to form a relationship with people who desire such things. It may be because of this that a gift is often more of a statement about the giver than one about the receiver. Further, Miller points out that women made most of the purchases in the area where he did fieldwork. Since the role of women in the modern nuclear family to a great extent consists of giving love and compassion to others, shopping activities are permeated by the same values. In addition, shopping is informed by the core Protestant value thrift; his informants compare their abilities to find items at reduced prices.

Miller's original depiction of the ethos of shopping is far removed from the much more pessimistic view typical of contemporary cultural criticism, which routinely associates shopping with selfish hedonism. Miller identifies some formerly neglected similarities between the forms of social integration in modern societies and in the traditional societies described by Mauss, Boas and others. This does not mean that Miller's theory is the only possible theory about shopping. With different ethnographic material, which included adolescents and single men, for example, he might have modified his conclusion. The point is none the less that he has demonstrated that shopping *can be* something entirely different from what many believe, and it is in this way that anthropological research can change our established views of the world.

AN INTERDISCIPLINARY PERSPECTIVE

One of the most striking recent developments regarding the scholarly attention to reciprocity, which testifies to its crucial place in human life, is the growing interest in reciprocity among scholars who belong to a totally different intellectual tradition from social and cultural anthropology. The great historical transformations described by Mauss and Polanyi are real, and have led to fundamental changes in the way of life and social organisation of the societies affected by them. But accepting this does not mean that *everything* has changed. The fact that it is possible for a western academic to understand, and translate credibly from, the life-worlds of peoples as far removed from his or hers as conceivable, indicates that humans have much in common everywhere.

During most of the twentieth century, the mainstream of social and cultural anthropology was concerned with the study of differences. American cultural relativism and the European tradition of studying small, stateless societies, along with the emphasis on comparison, encouraged researchers to look for differences rather than similarities. A century after the onset of Boas's reign, there are good reasons to question this almost singleminded emphasis on difference. Was not the ultimate aim of anthropology to reach an understanding of human universals? And was not the long journey of the discipline through the world of cultural difference in the final instance meant to lead to an understanding of Humanity with a capital H?

Many anthropologists agree that the answers to both questions is yes, but they then become hesitant. For it is far from easy to state what peoples have in common beyond banalities like 'humans are bipeds possessing verbal language'. For this reason, it is worth noting that there seems today to be wide agreement, not only among anthropologists, but also among biologically oriented scholars with an interest in human life, that reciprocity is a fundamental property of the human condition.

Maus, Polanyi and Sahlins took issue with a view of humans which assumed that they were individualistic, maximising and fundamentally selfish creatures. They associated this view with libertarianism and mainstream economics, but in other contexts, a similar view of 'man' as a fiercely competitive individualist has been associated with those of Darwin's adherents who claim that social and cultural phenomena must be understood within the framework of evolutionary theory. The slogans 'the struggle for survival' and 'the survival of the fittest', and the often uncritical use of the word 'competition' used to designate the dynamics of procreation and many other human activities, have been typical of Darwinist interpretations of humanity for generations. Against this background, it is astonishing that a growing number of sociobiologists and evolutionary psychologists now emphasise that cooperation, mutual trust and long-term reciprocity relations are evolutionarily adaptive. In a popular book which sums up the state of the art well, *The Origins of Virtue* (1996), science writer Matt Ridley shows how this can be. His argument is partly based on economic history and anthropology, but as a sociobiologist he also emphasises that recent mathematic models based on evolutionary assumptions show that cooperation 'pays off' in the long run. If one behaves like a selfish and insensitive rogue, one ends up with diminutive personal networks and few partners with whom to exchange things, services and intangibles.

Both evolutionary scientists and anthropologists, who approach the phenomena from very discrepant points of view, have, in other words, reached the conclusion that reciprocity, which creates enduring social bonds based on trust and mutual obligations, is a fundamental aspect of human life. As I shall try to show in the following chapters, this insight may be a good building-block for an anthropology whose ambitions include not only accounting for variation but also developing a vision of the universally human.

FURTHER READING

Davis, John (1992) *Exchange*. Buckingham: Open University Press.

Mauss, Marcel (1954) *The Gift*, tr. Ian Cunnison. London: Cohen and West.

Sahlins, Marshall (1972) *Stone Age Economics*. Chicago: University of Chicago Press.

6
Kinship

Since we have decided that reciprocity should be considered a fundamental dimension of social life, it goes without saying that the smallest unit we study in anthropology is not the single person, but the relationship between two. It is not the innermost thoughts of the individual that constitute our object of study, but the social dynamics between people and their products; where the innermost thoughts of the person, incidentally, are often expressed.

All societies contain some basic social groups. The concept *primary relationships* is often used to describe the closest and most enduring ties between persons. Many relationships of this kind are based on the overlapping institutions of kinship, family and household, but local communities and work relations can also provide a person with a strong and long-lived sense of personal belonging. There are, naturally, also other ways of organising primary relations; religious and political groups may play an important part, and some would also claim that the 'imagined community' of the nation can be a well-functioning surrogate for kin or family. In this chapter, which might have been called 'Social organisation' rather than 'Kinship', it would have been perfectly possible to write about the local community, the village or the household as a basic unit. The fact that the entire chapter is instead devoted to kinship, is due to a conviction that kinship lies at the base of the most viable forms of social organisation. This is certainly not always the case in a literal sense; kinship can often be extremely effective as a metaphor, and it is not true, as some overzealous adherents of biological explanations argue, that human acts can be explained with direct reference to their biological nature. Yet, it may be stated unequivocally that kinship and family are extremely basic, probably universal ways of thinking about, and organising, human belonging.

KINSHIP STUDIES

The last sentence may, at a glance, seem prosaic and pedestrian, bordering on the trivial. It is therefore not irrelevant to point out that such a statement is profoundly controversial in contemporary anthropology. Many anthropologists are on the verge of abandoning the concept entirely because, they argue, it does not travel well, that is to say it has no cross-culturally valid meaning. The concept of kinship as it has been used in anthropology since Morgan and Tylor, they argue, is ethnocentric and biologistic; it builds upon specific western ideas about kinship, and it is also based on notions about biological relatedness which dominate western society but not necessarily elsewhere. Although this critical attitude is necessary, evidence has not supported it well; a century of meticulous ethnographic research has shown that most peoples have similar (but far from identical) ways of thinking about kinship and blood relations.

In a review of the state of the art in kinship studies, Ladislav Holy (1996) commented some years ago that kinship was for many years a domain which anthropology could rightfully claim as its own. No other discipline in the social sciences or humanities studied kinship systematically. Among sociologists and psychologists there might be many who were interested in the family, but they covered only a tiny patch of the subject matter proper of anthropological studies of kinship. In the early 1950s, in the heyday of British structural-functionalism, kinship studies were in fact so dominant that outsiders spoke ironically of the subject as *kinshipology*. The situation has changed. At present, kinship studies form, quantitatively speaking, a relatively small branch of anthropology, although it remains an important one. In this chapter, I shall show why kinship studies have been a core activity in anthropology, how the field was weakened, and how it may rise to prominence again.

Although kinship studies are usually associated with British and European anthropology, it was an American, namely Lewis Henry Morgan, who established kinship as a distinct domain in the discipline. Through his broad explorations of cultural history and his fieldwork among the Iroquois in the mid-nineteenth century, Morgan became convinced that traditional societies were thoroughly organised on the basis of kinship and descent. Inheritance and property rights, political office and the composition of local communities were based on kinship; in societies which practised ancestor worship, even religion was based on kinship. Whereas our own complex societies built on an institutional differentiation with separate social institutions devoted to politics, economics, socialisation, law and so on, everything is fused in the idiom of kinship in traditional societies, according to Morgan and generations of anthropologists after him.

Morgan proposed several evolutionist explanatory accounts to understand and explain kinship, but the only one still to some extent in use, is his distinction between *classificatory* and *descriptive* kinship. In many societies, the same term is used to denote all the members of one's own kin group (which could be a clan) of the same gender and generation (e.g. words that might be translated as 'father' or 'sister'). In a classificatory system, the term would be identical for the father (F) as for the father's brother (FB), and for these brothers' first and second cousins. Descriptive systems distinguish terminologically between these kinds of kin, that is between *lineal* and *collateral* kin. However, classificatory terms also exist in descriptive systems. The word 'aunt' is an example from the English-speaking world, since she may be either the father's or mother's sister (FZ or MZ) or the spouse of the father's or mother's brother (FBW or MBW), or even, in societies which tolerate homosexual marriages, the spouse of one of their sisters (FZW or MZW). 'Sister-in-law' is similarly a classificatory term since she may be either the brother's wife (BW) or his wife's brother (WB). In descriptive systems it is never the less possible to denote, using descriptive terms, the exact relationship between one person and another person. When we say 'cousin', we may add 'my mother's sister's son' or 'my father's brother's daughter'.

Not only Morgan himself, but many of his contemporary cultural historians and anthropologists were fascinated by kinship. Most of them viewed it through an evolutionist lens. Some held that the transition from traditional to modern societies entailed a change from kinship to other principles as the foundation of social organisation, such as bureaucratic rule, parliamentarianism and – in the case of the individual – personal achievements. Maine's distinction between status and contract societies points in this direction. Morgan held, on his side, that societies had evolved from general promiscuity via matrilineal descent to patrilineal descent, an idea pursued further by the Swiss lawyer JB Bachofen. The fact that not only their own kind of society, but also very many 'primitive' ones, are cognatic was not taken into account.

Early in the twentieth century, kinship studies gradually became chiefly a European speciality, as social anthropologists (as opposed to the cultural anthropologists) were especially interested in understanding how societies worked, not how cultures were integrated. In order to achieve this, they soon realised that it was necessary to study systems of kinship, and they tended to see traditional societies as 'kinship based'. (It must never the less be noted that the one book Malinowski promised to write about the Trobrianders but never did, was the one about their kinship system. The most sophisticated kinship studies by the mid-twentieth century were carried out by associates of Radcliffe-Brown.) For several decades, moreover, kinship was virtually seen as identical to descent.

DESCENT

British social anthropology was firmly established as an academic discipline between the 1920s and the mid-1950s. In this period, structural-functionalism increasingly became the dominant theoretical mode of thought (especially after Radcliffe-Brown's return to England in 1937), and most of the important ethnographic studies in this school were based on research in Africa. Together, these two facts may explain why the descent model of kinship was nearly totally dominant in Anglophone anthropology for several decades.

In the introduction to the influential volume *African Political Systems* (1940), the editors Fortes and Evans-Pritchard divided African societies into three types: the small, decentralised bands of hunters and gatherers; the hierarchical and relatively centralised chiefdoms and kingdoms; and finally, the intermediate category of segmentary lineage societies. All three types were considered as having a kinship-based political organisation, but the editors were particularly interested in the segmentary societies. These societies were characterised by weak formal leadership, sometimes lacking recognised political leadership altogether. Sometimes they were described as *acephalous* ('headless') societies. Yet they seemed surprisingly stable and well-organised, and if the situation required it, they could mobilise great numbers of warriors.

The explanation, according to Fortes and Evans-Pritchard, was to be found in the peculiarities of the kinship-based social organisation. These societies were usually patrilineal. Each person belonged to a lineage consisting of persons who descended from the same ancestor. Within the lineage, classificatory kin terms were used; one term denoting brothers and first and second cousins, another denoting father and patrilateral uncles. The next level of organisation was the clan. It also consisted of persons who regarded themselves as the descendants of a shared ancestor, but the number of generations separating them was now such that they were no longer able to specify their genealogy in exact terms. The clan thus belonged to a systemic level above the lineage, and consisted of a number of lineages. Many of these societies were endogamous at the clan level and exogamous at the lineage level. This means that they were not allowed to marry within the lineage, but had to marry within the clan. (Clan exogamy, however, was also not uncommon.) At a yet higher level of social integration, the tribe as a whole was identified; that is, the people with a shared ethnonym and a common language and identity. (Some, such as Evans-Pritchard in his study of the Nuer, added yet another systemic level, that of the 'nation', which again consisted of several 'tribes'.)

Society is thus divided into segments operating at several levels; the lineage, the clan and the tribe. The size of such a segment depends on which systemic level the researcher is looking at – or, for the actors themselves – the current situation. When a conflict arises, the general Biblical principle applies 'it is me against my brother, my brother and I against our cousins, our cousins, my brother and I against our more remote relatives' and so on. The compass of the group is, in other words, situationally defined. It grows and shrinks according to need, one might say. The remarkable thing about the segmentary kin group is that it is completely decentralised and at the same time strongly integrated. There is scarcely any formal leadership, and the operational social community expands or shrinks according to need.

This model of unilineal, segmentary systems has been deeply influential in anthropology, and indeed may even today inspire scholars who study group identities. However, it has also been criticised and modified by other researchers. Some revisions of the descent model appeared in Laura and Paul Bohannan's research on the Tiv in Nigeria and Fredrik Barth's monograph about politics in Swat. Laura Bohannan showed, in 'A Genealogical Charter' (1952), that the Tiv actively manipulated genealogies to their own advantage (rights to property and land usage were genealogically determined), that is, individuals exploited the system for their own ends. It was thus not sufficient to study the system, but one also had to look at the use (and misuse) of it by individuals. This point recalls Firth's distinction between social structure and social organisation.

Barth showed that in the segmentary system in Swat, another patrilineal system, men would align themselves with remote relatives against their nearer relatives, that is the opposite of the situation in African societies. The reason was that there was competition over land, and the most attractive plots were the ones bordering on one's own. When a farmer tried to expand his fields, he would naturally look towards his neighbour, who would usually be a close relative because of the system of inheritance. In this case, segmentary organisation engendered fission at the lineage level and stimulated individualist entrepreneurship, quite contrary to what one might expect.

A more fundamental critique against the descent theory came, not unexpectedly, from Malinowski's students. Unlike the structural-functionalists, who loved abstract models with great comparative power, they had been taught to place the acting individual at the centre of analysis. Audrey Richards, who had studied the Bemba in northern Rhodesia (now Zambia), thus claimed that the elegant models applied by Evans-Pritchard on the Nuer existed almost nowhere but in the head of the anthropologist. In fact, she argued, people acted on the basis of a lot of different, sometimes conflicting alignments, and it was impossible to find the basis for the models in ongoing social life. One of Evans-Pritchards close allies, Max Gluckman (another leading Africanist), defended the model by showing that the many divergent groups any individual was a member of, in fact worked to integrate and mitigate conflict. The fact that a man both belonged to a lineage and lived in a village with several lineages present, meant that it was in his personal interest to avoid conflicts. Reality was, in other words, even more faithful to the structural-functionalist doctrine of integration than Evans-

Pritchard's original model implied. This, at any rate, seemed to be Gluckman's (1956) view.

Slightly later, John Barnes (1962), who had been trained as an Africanist, wrote an article about kinship in New Guinea. There, he showed that although kinship was important for local organisation, it did not function in the 'tidy' way it did in segmentary societies in Africa. Clans and lineages were dispersed over a much larger area, and loyalties tended to be local rather than based on kinship. His criticism, revealing further limitations of the descent model, was fairly fundamental. However, by this time, the theory of descent had already been challenged by a new, theoretically heavyweight theory, namely alliance theory.

ALLIANCE

In a sense, it is misleading to speak of alliance theory in this context. For the descent models developed by the British Africanists were to a great extent intended to show how alliances emerged; why stateless societies were not in a state of perpetual civil war, and how kinship served to lessen the risk of feud. Yet alliance theory is a conventional and largely acceptable term for describing the direction in kinship research which began in earnest when Lévi-Strauss published his *Les structures élémentaires de la parenté* (1949; trans. *The Elementary Structures of Kinship*, 1968), a voluminous and learned book which would have enduring consequences for the dominant ways of thinking about kinship.

Lévi-Strauss was, as noted before, influenced by the French sociological school of Durkheim and Mauss. He had also studied the new structural linguistics of the 1920s and 1930s, of which Ferdinand de Saussure and Roman Jakobson were, in different ways, the central theorists. This direction in linguistics emphasised *relationships* between sounds rather than the actual sounds, and Saussure established a distinction between *la langue* (language as a static resource, i.e. grammar, syntax, vocabulary) and *la parole* (language as actually spoken). Lévi-Strauss introduced both of these principles into anthropology. His book about kinship was more about marriage than about descent. In a famous passage, Lévi-Strauss claims that the beginning of society as such took place when a man for the first time in history gave his sister to another man. Because of the universal incest prohibition, he could not marry her himself, and thus *affinality* appeared, which is a strong bond of reciprocity which operates between persons who are not biologically related. In all societies which have been studied thoroughly, Lévi-Strauss argues, there are rules regulating who can marry whom. Many societies with classificatory kinship terminologies have two classes of persons belonging to opposite genders and the same generation: classificatory siblings and potential spouses. Either they are 'sisters' and 'brothers' or 'wives' and 'husbands'.

Lévi-Strauss distinguished between two kinds of rules regulating marriage practices, that is *prescriptive* and *preferential* ones, which correspond to strong and weak interpretations of the rules. However few, if any, prescriptive systems work in perfect accordance with the rules. Many societies in the Middle East and North Africa operate, as mentioned earlier, with a norm of FBD marriage (a male marries his father's brother's daughter) as a prescriptive principle, but in practice, the proportion of actual marriages conforming to the rule can be as low as 25 per cent.

Structuralist theory of kinship regards marriage in traditional societies as a form of group-based reciprocity, where the exchange concerns the 'super-gift', that is women. Later studies, not least those carried out by female anthropologists, have shown that this is a dubious generalisation. It is not necessarily the case that men exchange women; often, the power relations between the genders may be more equitable.

A central point in Lévi-Strauss's theory of kinship is never the less that marriage in traditional societies is group-based, and that it can be understood as a form of long-term reciprocity. Affinality creates stable alliances. When distinct kin groups (clans, moieties or other units that compose society) systematically exchange women, all of society becomes integrated through deep and long-lived commitments. In certain cases, one waits an entire generation before 'the gift' is reciprocated in the shape of another woman. In societies which practise transmission of bridewealth, it may occur that men work for their parents-in-law to fulfil their obligations virtually for the rest of their lives. Put differently, by marrying a particular woman, the man and his lineage commit themselves to working for the affinal family for years to come. This was the case among the Kachin, the Burmese highlanders studied by Edmund Leach. Their marriage system meant that the lineages who became wife-givers (*mayu*) were higher-ranking than the lineages who received wives (*dama*), and this relationship was confirmed in that the bridewealth had to be 'paid' over many years. Men thus had a lower rank than their parents-in-law, expressed through their enduring debt relationship.

Following the introduction of Lévi-Strauss' alternative account of kinship, there ensued a period of debate between descent theorists and defenders of the alliance theory. The bond of marriage had not been neglected by the British Africanists, but to them, the descent group was the corporate unit, that is the politically unified group 'acting as one'; and women were rarely perceived as independent agents. Descent was a peripheral theme for Lévi-Strauss, who was far more interested in discovering the 'grammar' that regulated the flow of women in different societies. In more recent kinship studies, there is no explicit conflict between the two perspectives, which are rather seen as offering complementary insights. Few would deny that if kinship is a meaningful term, both marriage and descent are important components of it.

KINSHIP AND FAMILY

The distinction between descent and alliance (affinality) leads us to another distinction, which is not commonly invoked in everyday ideas about kinship. The point here is that kinship and family ties may refer to two rather different kinds of institution. Kinship usually refers to the descent group. It can be unilineal (patri- or matrilineal) or cognatic/bilateral. Western societies are based on a cognatic principle, although the patrilateral aspect has been given some priority, for example, in some European countries, only male offspring have been allowed to inherit farmland, and in most European countries, family surnames still tend to follow the male side (although there have been recent changes in a few places).

The term 'family' normally refers to the household, that is, the group which lives under the same roof and usually shares the main meal of the day. The family usually consists of people related to each other through kinship, as well as people who are not related. This would be the case even in the small nuclear family, the typical household form in western society. A man is kin to his children, but not to his wife, although they all belong to the same family. In a patrilineal society, the mother would not even belong to the same kin group as her children, but to the same group as her brother and his children.

There are several distinct kinds of family. The minimal form, which is far from unknown in western societies, but which also exists in many other parts of the world, consists of one adult (usually a woman) and her or his children. A more common form is the nuclear family, that is a couple and their children; and in addition, anthropologists may distinguish between several variants of what is commonly known as extended families. Many consist of a nuclear family plus one of the spouses' parents and any of their unmarried siblings; some are 'joint' families consisting of the nuclear families of two or more siblings; and there are other forms, where, for example, all male members of a lineage and their spouses and children live under the same roof.

When we emphasise that kinship and family are not the same thing, it is not due to a mere wish to keep things separate. It is no coincidence that an astonishing number of societies have jokes involving mothers-in-law. The relationships engaged in by this kind of affine are often a source of tensions, and some readers may find solace in the fact that the problem of mothers-in-law is a structural one.

Mothers have, in most societies, comprehensive ties of reciprocity with their sons and daughters. When the children marry, this tie is transformed and often weakened, since the spouses now lay claim to a chunk of the social world which used to be regulated by descent (the mother–child relationship). There thus emerges competition between spouse and mother for the attention and loyalty of the daughter or son, which frequently appears as chronic, if simmering, conflict. Jokes are told, for example, about confrontations between the mother and the young wife; the latter detests the older woman's interfering manner, while the former mistrusts the young woman's ability to care properly for her son. Tearful letters to editors of women's weeklies from mothers who suspect that the young husband mistreats their little girl express similar tensions. Both men and women feel slightly invaded by mothers-in-law, while the mothers-in-law, on their part, claim rights to continuity in their relationship with their children, and demand what they regard as their right in relation to their grandchildren.

THEORY AND PRACTICE

It was mentioned above that no society has a prescriptive *practice*. The rules are always adjusted to fit the bumpy and contradictory world of experience. It must never the less be admitted that absolute rules exist everywhere. The incest prohibition exists in all societies, even if it has often been pointed out that it varies in its significance and compass; in some societies, it is limited to the kin we might call close family, that is persons with the same biological mother and father and their relatives in direct lines of descent; but usually, half-siblings are included in the incest prohibition, and often the prohibition is extended to include what we might call more remote relatives. In certain societies – ancient Egypt is the most famous – marriage between brother and sister has been accepted, and not just among the royalty. As a general rule we may say that violations of the incest prohibition or 'taboo' tend to be punished severely. Incest and sex with children belong to the diminishing category of forms of sexual behaviour which are almost universally condemned in western societies after the 'sexual liberation' which accelerated after the invention of the pill in the 1960s. In most affairs to do with kinship (including sex), practices tend to be more flexible than the rules suggest, or the rules themselves can be stretched through imaginative interpretations.

Let us take the principle of virilocality as an example. This rule states, in many patrilineal societies, that the new household formed through marriage should be tied to the husband's father and his household, either by moving into this household (sometimes resulting in the wife being treated more or less like a maid), or by establishing their own household in the immediate vicinity of the husband's family. Research has indicated that this rule is often followed no more closely than the rule prescribing FBD marriage in western Asia. A researcher who studied Finnish Sami concluded that the rule of virilocality could not exist there, since only a small proportion of the newly-weds actually moved in with the husband's family. The fact is that the rule did exist, but practices were regulated by innumerable pragmatic considerations making most households exceptions. For the rule to continue to function, it was sufficient that it be followed in a limited number of cases, making it possible to uphold it as an ideal and perpetuating alliances. Since rules of this kind (FBD marriages, virilocality, etc.) are meant to maintain alliances and social stability, it is sufficient that, for example, one of five brothers marries his patrilateral cousin. That would ensure the continuance of the alliance for the next generation.

Selective use of kinship relations is very widespread, contributing to the view of kinship as a social construction. Most of us presumably find ourselves occasionally in the same situation as the North African mule, who spoke incessantly about his uncle, the horse, but who never mentioned his father, the donkey. Of the many actual relatives each of us has – the number grows dramatically in many cases if one opts to include affines – probably, only a small proportion are regularly invoked. They would include the relatives we are in regular contact with, or who we consider it strategically beneficial to emphasise. In societies where kinship still creates strong obligations of reciprocity, successful persons may occasionally hear a knock on the door, only to discover that the stairway is crammed with dimly familiar faces who cheerfully address them as 'uncle'.

Kinship builds upon two complementary principles: descent and marriage. But both can be manipulated and fiddled with, by natives as well as by anthropologists. There exists a considerable critical literature about kinship; some of it was mentioned briefly at the beginning of this chapter, and we now turn to a slightly more detailed examination.

The renowned American anthropologist David Schneider tried for years, through his own research and that of his students, to demonstrate that anthropological thinking about kinship was fundamentally flawed in its ethnocentric and biologistic bias. It is debatable whether he succeeded in showing this. All or nearly all peoples have cultural notions to the effect that everybody has a father and a mother, and that the parent–child bond is important. Ideas about blood relatedness vary, but they are usually strong, even if the social role of the father may be relatively unimportant in matrilineal societies, and adopted children may be treated in exactly the same way as biological offspring. A notion which exists in many societies is that the hard, dry body parts (chiefly the skeleton) are inherited from the father, while the soft, wet and perishable body parts are inherited from the mother. Such ideas vary from society to society, but there seems to be fairly widespread cross-cultural agreement that children have something in common with their parents, to put it mildly. Just what this might be, and whether the parents need to be biological parents in order to have this 'something in common' with their children, is another question which will be touched upon in a little while.

The concept of marriage, too, has been subjected to criticism along the same lines as Schneider's critique of the concept of kinship. Edmund Leach, like Rodney Needham after him, claimed that it was impossible to make a list of criteria defining marriage which would be acceptable everywhere. As a conclusion, they claimed that marriage does not exist as a cross-culturally valid category; the bond between a man and woman who have children together varies so much in content that it cannot be designated with the same term everywhere.

Personally, I must confess to being only moderately impressed by this kind of criticism. It is not difficult to show that everything on Earth is unique; in the final instance every individual interprets the world in their own idiosyncratic way. Often it is intellectually necessary, and it can even be politically urgent, to demonstrate that life-worlds are constructed locally and in fact are deeply divergent; all the inhabitants on Earth do not dream of becoming a kind of North American. At the same time, the critiques of the concepts of kinship and marriage seem overly pedantic, almost quarrelsome. Shouldn't one instead conclude that it is almost incredible, but true, that in virtually all societies on Earth, which are extremely different from each other in most ways, there exist some ideas about ties of commitment between men and women and their shared children, and some practical devices – rules, ideas, practices – enabling them to handle these relationships in conventionalised and predictable ways; and that these resemble each other quite a bit, in spite of enormous differences in other areas?

BIOLOGY AND KINSHIP

This much said, it seems that an explicit treatment of the relationship between kinship and biology is inevitable. Needham, Schneider and the anthropologists who agree with them, tend to deny that biology has anything to do with kinship at all.

To them, what governs human interaction amounts to cultural constructions, full stop. Others accord biology a varying degree of importance for kinship, but are often implicit or vague. In this section, I shall try to be explicit. Biology influences kinship in two ways: subjectively and objectively. We must distinguish carefully between these levels of signification in order to avoid misunderstandings in the treatment of this controversial area.

When biology influences kinship subjectively, it happens through cultural notions about blood relatedness and its implication, notions which are connected to practices. If a biological father has certain rights *vis-à-vis* his children, even if they were raised by another man ('stepfather'), it is because there is general agreement that biological relatedness exists independently of social experience. Even if he has never met his children, he is assumed to have a special relationship to them. In many countries, however, the so-called *pater est* principle has been predominant in family law. It states that whoever has functioned as a father during the upbringing of the child is considered the child's father, even if it should become apparent that he is not the child's biological father. (Studies indicate that a small number of the children who are born in western European societies have another biological father than the one living with the child's mother, even if this is unknown to the *pater*.) In recent years, as DNA testing has made it possible to decide beyond reasonable doubt whether or not a *pater* (social father) is also *genitor* (biological father), there has been a renewed interest in this question, not least among men who fear that they have been cuckolded at crucial moments in their cohabitation.

Not all peoples hold the same views about the biological significance of kinship. In many parts of the world, such as Polynesian islands, adoption is widespread, and it is regarded as unproblematic. Even in western Europe and North America, adoption of children from less economically developed countries has become more common in recent years. The adopted children are, culturally speaking, 100 per cent western, but they have a visibly different genetic origin. Adopted children are often asked about their origins, especially in societies with few immigrants, and when they answer, for example, 'Lübeck', the follow-up question might be, 'But where are you *really* from?' The use of the word 'really' is interesting in this context, since it indicates that cultural notions exist about a biological substratum which is relevant to identity even if it is not connected to their social experience. Although no respected scholars believe that culture 'is in the blood' any more, it seems that a similar folk notion continues to exist.

Cultural notions about the significance of biology for kinship exist nearly everywhere. Assumptions to the effect that children inherit personality traits from their parents are very common. Slightly less common, but widespread in certain parts of the world, is the idea that children are reborn ancestors and ancestresses. Proverbs of the generic 'blood is thicker than water' kind exist in otherwise very different societies, but the practical and conceptual implications of these notions vary.

Concerning the view that biology influences kinship objectively, this is also a widespread view among researchers, but it has never been particularly popular among sociocultural anthropologists. The people who advocate this view usually have their background in the natural sciences, or they belong to disciplines which aspire to the kind of accuracy sometimes found in the natural sciences (e.g. certain parts of psychology and linguistics). The most influential, and arguably the most interesting, biological interpretation of kinship is the one which forms part of the great and diverse heritage of Darwin and his theory of evolution.

Some researchers, who are called sociobiologists or, increasingly, evolutionary psychologists, hold that biological explanations will make it easier to understand social and cultural dynamics. They assume, incidentally like many anthropologists, that most people don't know exactly why they do whatever it is that they do. But unlike the anthropologists, they do not look to social circumstances or historical events for the explanation, but in humanity's identity as a mammal. A central feature of the sociobiological account of kinship is the concept of *kin selection*. According to this principle, individuals of any species, including homo sapiens, would be inclined to behave in a supporting and unselfish way towards close biological kin. The reason is that they share most of their genetic material with their siblings, parents and cousins. Thus, phenomena such as nepotism (favourable treatment of kin) seem to have a biological explanation. If I cannot spread my own genes, then at least I can help my cousins or siblings to spread theirs.

Kin selection has been studied in a number of ways. One of the most famous studies is Martin Daly and Margo Wilson's book *Homicide* (1988), an investigation of the frequency of murder of own children, based on statistical material from several countries. Their conclusion is that the risk of this happening rises dramatically if the children are not one's own biological offspring. Stepfathers represent a disproportionally high ratio of these murders. The explanation, faithful to the tenets of evolutionary theory, is that stepfathers are likely to behave in this way since they do not have any biological interest in 'investing' in children to whom they are not genetically close.

There has been considerable debate about Daly and Wilson's conclusions. In this context, it is sufficient to point out that the book does not explain everything. For example, it is an unexplained fact that adoptive fathers hardly ever murder their adopted children, even if they are genetically even more remote from their children than the stepfathers usually are from theirs. Could this discrepancy perhaps be explained by looking at differences in social circumstances and external pressure on the family? Stepfathers tend to be in a more precarious situation than adoptive fathers, who have often been screened for 'suitability' by the authorities and who tend to live in stable, middle-class relationships. Conversely, history is rife with examples of men who have produced numerous offspring without displaying much interest in 'parental investment' in them. The most obvious example would be slave owners who made female slaves pregnant; in most cases, they did not even admit their paternity. In situations of war, it does not seem to be a problem for invading armies that their use of mass rape as a method of humiliation leads to a large number of pregnancies where the fathers will never meet their children. So much, it seems, for the idea that biological relatedness guarantees a privileged, close and mutually committing relationship.

Is kinship ultimately nature or culture? The question is wrongly stated, for as the next chapter will indicate, neither pure nature nor pure culture exists. Like most human phenomena, kinship is a stew of nature and culture, where it is difficult to separate the ingredients. It is also, as the preceding discussions have indicated, both universal and locally unique.

KINSHIP IN MODERN SOCIETIES

It is a common assumption that kinship is exceptionally important in traditional societies, and becomes less and less important as the societies 'develop', becoming larger and more complex. The state, the anonymous labour market, the monetary economy, the mass media and, above all, individualism seem to replace kin and family in one area after another. It is no coincidence that some of the most passionate debates about migrants in western Europe concern the relationship of immigrants to their kin and family. For years, the close family ties characteristic of many immigrants, particularly from Asia, were regarded in western public spheres as a positive trait, but since the late 1990s, media stories increasingly report phenomena such as enforced marriages, authoritarian treatment of children and honour killings. The tightly integrated kin group, which is able to act corporatively (the group acts as if it were one subject), now seems, in the eyes of many, not to be compatible with the individualism and freedom valued by modern society.

It is difficult to argue against the view that kinship is generally less important in modern societies than in traditional ones. The first modern sociologists and anthropologists, who wrote in the mid-nineteenth century, had already noticed that the industrial revolution had weakened the ties of kinship and family. Closer to the present, sociologists have been speaking about the 'emptying of functions' in the family; several of the traditional tasks of the family are now taken on by the school and the public sector, and anthropologists who write about modern societies have usually been relatively unconcerned with kinship (with a few remarkable exceptions, such as David Schneider and Marilyn Strathern). Unless, that is, they write about ethnic minorities.

Yet it is necessary to oppose the common, simplistic view. When stateless societies are described as 'kinship based societies', the term is nearly always a misleading exaggeration. It may be correct that kinship regulates marriage practices, political power and land distribution in those societies, but it never happens in a mechanical way; individual strategies always play an important part, and besides, considerations which have nothing to do with kinship are also invariably relevant. In addition, and conversely, it is becoming increasingly evident that kinship continues to play an important part in modern societies. Studies of local communities in western Europe and North America confirm that many social networks are kinship-based, and that significant resources flow through them. It can be anything from help in jobseeking to the exchange of services between brothers-in-law. The social networks of many are never tighter, more existentially important and filled with meaning than during collective, kinship-based events such as Christmas parties and vacations at family properties. In addition, studies of adoption and artificial insemination reveal that kinship and family are crucial elements of personal identity. At a more trivial and obvious level, there is no doubt that family background is an important factor in determining career opportunities. So although kinship, in this kind of society, does not regulate everything from economic activities and marriage to place of residence and value outlooks, there is no reason to assume that it is so unimportant that anthropologists who study these societies can afford to neglect it. There are good reasons to claim that the tension between family, kinship and individual freedom is one of the most fascinating and researchable aspects of modern society, and considering the level of detailed knowledge we already possess about kinship in remote areas, anthropology is in a perfect position to say something about the wider significance of kinship, encompassing the 'post-kinship based societies' as well as the traditional ones.

In the discussion about biology and kinship above, it might seem that it makes no difference whether cultural notions about biological relatedness are true or false. In fact, in anthropological research, the job consists of discovering what the native ideas are, how they connect to social practices and the relative stability or change in society, and how ideas and practices are in turn connected with structural features and cultural patterns which are not immediately available for observation. It is not the task of anthropologists to give our informants marks according to their ability to conform to our own ideas about the world. When the context of discouse shifts from professional concerns to political ones, the situation necessarily changes, but it may none the less be useful to spend some time understanding the world before trying to change it. What evidently annoyed anthropologists like Schneider and Needham was that so many of their colleagues had uncritically adopted Morgan's distinction between classificatory and descriptive kinship, as if 'our' way of thinking about kinship was somehow more accurate (more 'descriptive') than the prevalent ideas in societies with classificatory kinship.

The critics of kinship theory hold that since kinship is always influenced by local views of biology and affinity, and since they vary, one should leave bias behind as far as possible in order to be prepared to take in the facts on the ground as accurately as one can. This is an important point. In recent years, there has been a great deal of promising research gravitating around the concept of *the house* as an analytical category, especially among south-east Asianists. The house has a significance in parts of this cultural area which is reminiscent of the old trading houses of Europe. It is connected to a family name, but membership of the house can be achieved in a number of different ways; through marriage, descent, friendship, professional services or personal qualities. Janet Carsten, who has devoted much attention to the house, suggests, by way of a conclusion, that the concept of kinship may perhaps be replaced by a concept of *relatedness*, which lacks the unfortunate biological connotations of the kinship concept.

This point of view is less convincing in my view, and it smacks of dilution. The relationships between mother, father and children, family trees and genealogies, preferential treatment of relatives and alliances through marriage furnish us with some of the few really good and useful comparative concepts we have in anthropology. They exist everywhere in one form or another, and they differ in interesting ways. If the ultimate goal is to discover the unity of humanity through its manifold appearances, the profession cannot afford to let go of the still rich gold mine of kinship.

FURTHER READING

Holy, Ladislav (1996) *Anthropological Perspectives on Kinship*. London: Pluto.
Schneider, David (1968) *American Kinship: A Cultural Account*. Englewood Cliffs: Prentice-Hall.

7
Nature

For more than 100 years, the relation between the social sciences and the natural sciences has been fraught with difficulties. A minority of social scientists (including some anthropologists) regard their activity as an extension, or a branch, of biological research. A possibly somewhat larger group believe that the social sciences ought to be sciences *of the same kind* as the natural sciences; that they should strive after the same kind of precision and the same kind of parsimonious clarity which can be achieved for instance in chemistry. Radcliffe-Brown defended this positivist view in his day, and his last, posthumously published book was called *A Natural Science of Society*. However, a majority of social and cultural anthropologists regard their professional activities as being markedly different from the natural sciences. Whereas mainstream biology, for example, seeks unequivocality and general laws, most anthropologists accept that the worlds we study are complex and ambiguous, and that even an outstanding ethnographic study of, say, the Tiv or the Nuer, can never offer the last word about these peoples. It is always possible to show new connections and patterns, and to produce new angles resulting in new ethnography. Sometimes, one is faced with the impression that biology and anthropology produce forms of knowledge which are fundamentally different from each other. They raise different kinds of question and offer answers which make statements about qualitatively different aspects of the world.

Many may object that this view is far too pessimistic. Shouldn't we rather try to build bridges across the gulf separating discrete traditions seeking knowledge, trying to create a unitary understanding which encompasses knowledge about human biology, history and its cultural specificity alike? The answer is in principle yes, but in practice the task may not be so easy. This chapter indicates how anthropology deals with nature, highlighting both parallels, convergences and divergences from biological perspectives. Although the account is necessarily partial, it will become clear that the contribution of anthropology consists, among other things, of showing that things are more complex than they seem.

INNER NATURE

Two kinds of nature are dealt with in anthropological thought, namely inner and outer nature. The inner one amounts to human nature, while the outer or external nature is the ecology which encompasses us and of which we are a part. Both are parts of the great tree of life, but in the professional literature they tend to be dealt with in different bodies of research. Anthropological studies devoted to human nature (or lack of such) tend to take their point of departure in theories about universal traits of humanity as a species, and discuss them in the light of diverse (or highly selective) empirical material. Studies of outer nature, on the contrary, concentrate on showing how culture and society are influenced by, and stand in a dynamic relationship to, their ecological surroundings. This line of research, often labelled human ecology, does not necessarily take a stance in relation to theories of human nature.

Modern sociology and anthropology were founded by theorists who, with a few exceptions, sharply rejected common generalisations, inside and outside of science, about 'human nature'. Marx once wrote that even the human sensory apparatus was a product of history, that is that humans in most respects are shaped by society and not by an inborn nature. Durkheim argued passionately and polemically against explanations which referred to an unchangeable human nature; in one of his best books, he showed that the suicide rate varies systematically because of what we might today call cultural differences, and in his book about religious forms, he argues that mental illness is clearly caused by social conditions. Boas was an important critic – probably *the* most important critic – of the racist pseudoscience dominating public life at the outset of his career in the late nineteenth century. His efforts, disseminated through academic and popular writings alike, aimed at showing that differences in thought patterns and apparent abilities which existed systematically between different groups, were caused by cultural and not innate variations. Although he encountered much opposition from powerful forces inside and outside the academy, Boas' views ultimately prevailed.

Among the exceptions, Morgan and Tylor are the most obvious. Morgan saw no qualitative difference between humans and (other) animals, and wrote, in his book about 'the American beaver and his works', in a passage cited approvingly by Darwin, that the intelligence of the beaver was of the same kind as human intelligence. What he could have meant by this is hard to fathom; we are certain that beavers do not distinguish between classificatory and descriptive kinship. As regards Tylor, he assumed that 'man' had a number of inborn qualities which were expressed through culture, and his relationship with Darwin was one of mutual respect and influence. Darwin himself wrote a couple of thought-provoking books about human nature, but he had no consistent view of the relationship between culture and nature. In principle, he saw culture as a part of nature, but he never tried to deny that there were cultural values and practices which clearly counteracted the central principle governing natural processes, that is the struggle for survival (and reproduction). One example was the Christian virtue of loving one's neighbour. Darwin was also worried that the culture of his era seemed to remove humans from their nature, through women's liberation for example, and he thereby admitted indirectly that culture possessed a certain degree of autonomy *vis-à-vis* nature.

The dominant schools in the anthropology of most of the twentieth century offered little space for the exploration of human nature, with the partial exception of structuralism. British anthropology gave primacy to society; social conditions required sociological explanations, and there was little reason to look to nature for causes. American anthropology regarded culture more or less as *sui generis* (self-producing) and was generally hostile towards attempts at explaining culture biologically. French anthropology was indebted to Durkheim and Mauss, and the main tendency has been to see human nature as a cultural construction rather than as something existing in itself. This does not mean that leading anthropologists rejected biological research or Darwinian theory, but that they saw the findings of biology as irrelevant for the study of culture and society. According to them, biological evolution was essential in accounting for the species development of humans until the advent of culture (language, rituals, etc.). From then on, culture quickly acquired its own dynamics, and thus developed independently of the much slower biological evolution.

The exceptions and points of contact are many. Malinowski's functionalism was based on a home-made list of 'universal human needs', which different cultures in his view satisfied in culturally specific ways. Lévi-Strauss's structuralism is a doctrine about universal, objective aspects of the human mind, and even Durkheim's sociology and Radcliffe-Brown's adaptation of it presuppose some common mental traits, for if all societies follow the same 'social laws', there must be something about the human condition which ensures this congruence between societies that have never been in mutual contact. The entire discipline of social and cultural anthropology builds on the principle of the mental unity of humanity, that is that all humans are born with roughly the same cognitive equipment. Yet it is correct, as some critics have pointed out in recent years, that anthropology has been partly based on an implicit theory about human nature, and that it has also claimed that it is human nature to be unnatural; that is, our inborn faculties and potentials only provide us with a few, vague and general dispositions, and that they can be shaped in nearly any direction. Be this as it may, it is clear that most anthropologists have, for more than 100 years, been more interested in culturally induced variation than in biologically underpinned similarities.

That important questions are at stake here, is evident through the old debate about aggression. The story is, briefly, this. Since the breakthrough of Darwinism in the second half of the nineteenth century, many Darwinists (but not all) have assumed that animals, in particular males, are forced to act aggressively in situations which threaten the survival of themselves and their offspring. Those who believe that Darwinism is valid in an undiluted form when the subject matter is humanity as well (and they are a smaller crowd, even if publicly very visible), thus assume that humans, again in particular male humans, have an inborn tendency for aggression. It becomes apparent in situations of rivalry between individuals concerning female favours, and in group competition over scarce resources. Killing and war are assumed, in accordance with this theory, to be rooted in our animal nature.

Against this view, anthropologists on both sides of the Atlantic have argued that cross-cultural variations are such that it makes little sense to appeal to human nature for an explanation of violence and 'aggression'. Why is the murder rate so much higher among San people in southern Africa than among Ainu in Japan? Why is the murder rate in Detroit many times higher than in neighbouring Hamilton (on the other side of the Canadian border)? Such variations require historical and sociological explanations, they argue, not biological ones. The geneticist Steve Jones discusses, in one of his popular books (Jones 1996), the theory that the high murder rate in the big cities of the USA is somehow connected with innate male aggression, and he simply asks why there are so many fewer murders in large British cities like London. The question can largely be answered simply by pointing out that there are far more handguns in the USA than in Britain. Jones, who is far from hostile towards genetic accounts – he makes his living from them – also reflects on alcoholism in an interesting way. For some years, it has been common to assume that alcoholism may have a genetic component, meaning in tabloid language that 'alcoholism is hereditary'. The genetic pattern which is believed to make its bearers susceptible to alcoholism is fairly evenly distributed across societies. It then turns out, of course, that alcoholism is widespread in Britain, but nearly non-existent in Iran (where it is very difficult to acquire alcohol). Should we then, Jones asks, draw the conclusion that alcoholism is hereditary in Britain but not in Iran? Of course not; the point is that innate dispositions can only become operative through the appropriate interaction with the environment, which in the case of humans is largely sociocultural.

This kind of critique of the sociobiological perspective is a mild variety. Here, it is accepted that a human nature exists and is relatively fixed, but that it disposes for a great number of traits and behaviours, only a few of which are allowed to flourish, due to the constraints and incentives of the environment. Inborn potentials for hunting abilities are realised in the Amazon but not in Ireland; and inborn potentials for composition came to fruition in the Salzburg bourgeoisie of the mid-eighteenth century, but hardly in the Siberia of the same period.

A more radical critique would claim that the very idea of humans possessing a great number of specific innate potentials or dispositions is erroneous. Several anthropological books about aggression which defend this view have been published over the years. One of the more recent ones is the edited collection *Societies at Peace* (Howell and Willis 1989), where the contributors argue that there is no empirical basis for claiming that aggression is inborn. They describe societies, like the Chewong in the Malay peninsula studied by Howell, where there isn't even a word that can reasonably be translated as 'aggression'. The editors' conclusion is that humans have inborn dispositions for *sociality*, that is cooperation and reciprocity, but not for aggression.

We should take note of the fact that even these critics, who disagree strongly (sometimes aggressively) with those who claim that it is human nature to be aggressive, conclude that humans do indeed possess certain innate qualities, in this case sociality. They thereby follow solid Durkheimian tradition, but they also defend a view which is in fact compatible with an interpretation of Darwinism which emphasises cooperation rather than competition as the most evolutionarily advantageous quality. This was the view of, amongst others, Alfred Russel Wallace, Darwin's contemporary and co-founder of the theory of evolution by natural selection.

There is by now a considerable professional literature about emotions in both anthropology and ethology (the study of animal behaviour). Darwin was one of the first to take advantage of cross-cultural findings when theorising about human emotions, in a book from 1872. This book contains an interesting discussion of blushing, which shows that the questions raised by biologists and anthropologists are frequently of different kinds. Darwin regards blushing as a uniquely human emotion, that is a form of emotional behaviour which does not exist among other species. (The non-English reader cannot but add that it is also a culturally specific behaviour related to that extremely English emotion, *embarrassment!*) He then goes through the available material on blushing among different peoples, and discovers that all peoples seem to blush. A problem then arises in the treatment of a particular Amazon tribe. They did not appear to blush, although they walked around naked. However, they were granted a lengthy visit from European missionaries, and lo and behold; after a year they began to blush, just like the rest of us. Darwin's conclusion is that this change proves that blushing is universal, every human being is able to blush, hence blushing is innately human.

In opting for this interpretation, Darwin misses a golden opportunity to say something interesting about the relationship between nature and culture. What he shows is, in fact, that embarrassment and blushing are *cultural* phenomena, since at least one people exists which does not initially possess the faculty of blushing. Moreover, he could have concluded that all humans have an inborn potential for blushing, but that they do not necessarily use it! This insight might then have been used as a stepping-stone to other domains of human activity. We all possess a great number of innate dispositions, but we only use a few of them; and which of them are developed, and how they are developed, depends on the society we live in. With this kind of starting-point, Darwin and his successors could have studied both human universals and cultural variation without reducing one to the other.

Unfortunately, intellectual life in the twentieth century would take a different direction. Instead of a perspective highlighting the dynamic interaction between nature and culture, there have been entrenched conflicts contrasting 'nature and nurture' right through the century. And anthropologists have often taken the frontline, usually on the 'nurture' side of the equation. Instead of a 'both-and' understanding, the outcome has usually been a stalemate of the 'either-or' kind.

EXTERNAL NATURE

Explorations of the relationship between ecology and society, which had not been a major priority to the Boas school, saw a healthy reinvigoration in American anthropology just after the Second World War. In British social anthropology, the study of ecology and society has been a more marginal speciality for many decades, although there are important contemporary anthropologists in Britain, like Tim Ingold, who combine ecological concerns with a more experience-near anthropology. In France, a similar situation exists, where important studies, like Philippe Descola's work from the Amazon, are based in part on an ecological understanding, but as in Britain, most French anthropology sees nature either as a cultural construction or not at all. It should be noted here that in Evans-Pritchard's structural-functionalist benchmark study *The Nuer*, an ample part of the analysis is devoted to ecological conditions, which were then seen as an important part of the structural framework. Of his contemporaries, Darryl Forde at University College London was almost alone in continuing to incorporate ecology in sociocultural anthropology.

Let us return to the USA of the early postwar years. The young rebels who regarded material factors as fundamental to human life – Julian Steward and Leslie White – were enthusiastic about the new science of ecology, and quickly saw its potential contribution to research about culture. The new, interdisciplinary field of human ecology was established in the 1950s, its aim being to study human activity as ecological adaptation. Especially in studies of societies with a simple technology – hunter-gatherers, horticulturalists – the perspectives offered by human ecology have been popular. Such studies have often been carried out with the help of quantitative methods, and the areas investigated have often included energy exploitation and resource dynamics. Such concerns can be traced back to Marx (or even further), who held the view that superstructure (the non-material aspects of culture and society) was largely determined by the infrastructure (property relations and technology). Marx was never the less hostile to ecological explanations, which he saw as politically reactionary since they did not take the liberating potential of technological change into account. Just as later Marxists have proposed many, often clever and intricate solutions to the infrastructure–superstructure problem, human ecologists (or cultural ecologists) have proposed many different models of the relationship between the material and the symbolic. Both Steward and White regarded symbolic culture as relatively autonomous; it might take several paths, and was far from totally determined by ecology and technology. Steward's distinction between the cultural core and the rest of culture (which included everything from law and kinship to art and language) implied that there was no simple, deterministic relationship between the two. White gauged the degree of cultural evolution by looking at the amount of available energy that was harnessed by human activity, and he thus saw clear connections between energy exploitation ad social complexity. On the other hand, White also held that symbolic culture – ideology, religion and so on – was largely autonomous.

This cluster of issues is both old and complex. A couple of famous examples may illustrate how it has been dealt with in practice. Of Steward and White's successors, Marvin Harris has been the most visible and controversial one. His theoretical programme, cultural materialism (not to be confused with the cultural materialism of Raymond Williams), is both more ambitious and more deterministic than those of his predecessors. In Harris' view, symbolic culture and anything else that might be included in Steward's blanket term 'the rest of culture' were by and large created by the material level. Harris, who died in 2001, wrote many books, but his most famous article arguably remains his aforementioned piece about sacred cows in India. Harris enlists a number of arguments for his view that the Indian cows are sacred for ecological and economic reasons, not for religious reasons as most Indians believe. The untethered Indian cows, who tend to wander freely around streets and curbs, subsist on rubbish and marginal grass which would otherwise have gone to waste. The milk is used as human nourishment (Indians, like northern Europeans and North Americans, are devoted milk-drinkers); the excrements are used for anything from manure to housebuilding, and when a cow eventually dies, the hide is turned into leather by ritually impure specialists, and even the meat is eaten by people who rank so low on the Hindu scale of ritual purity that the prohibition on beef does not apply to them. In other words, Harris concludes, the cows are *de facto* sacred because it is economically and ecologically sensible to keep it that way, and the religious notions about the sacred status of the cow are there because they are functional.

This kind of explanation appeared to be elegant and full of insight to many who encountered it when it was published. But it has serious problems. If the sacred cow is so functional in India, why do sacred animals of similar kinds not exist everywhere? Most food prohibitions, besides, do not appear to be ecologically rational. There is no ecological or economic reason that we should not eat human flesh. The late, famous killer whale Keiko, known through the film *Free Willy*, could have given a nourishing meal to 5000 hungry Sudanese, but because of the widespread cultural prohibition on whale meat in the western world, this was an unthinkable scenario. (Keiko, who died of old age in one of the few countries in the world where whale meat is eaten, namely Norway, was buried on the shore following his death.) And, as Marshall Sahlins – a former student of White, now a theoretical antagonist of Harris – has pointed out, why was there a popular outcry in California when horse meat was introduced in the supermarkets?

These examples illustrate the same general point as the discussion about Darwin and blushing above. All societies depend on developing institutions that contribute to the maintenance of society. The options are limited by ecological conditions, technology and population density. But of all the potential options in a society, only a minuscule number are actually exploited. In addition, it is undoubtedly true that not everything in a society is 'functional'. As Lévi-Strauss expressed it in a rather overbearing comment on Malinowski: 'Saying that societies function is trivial. But stating that everything in a society is functional, is absurd.' Humans give meaning to life in ways that make life more difficult, and society less well integrated, than necessary.

The most widely discussed study of the relationship between ecology and culture is a book about pigs and rituals in highland New Guinea. The author was Roy Rappaport, and the book, *Pigs for the Ancestors*, was first published in 1967, and then in a vastly expanded edition, furnished with the author's many additional thoughts and responses to critics, in 1984. Rappaport's analysis went as follows. Like many other highland peoples, the Tsembaga are horticulturalists who also keep pigs. About once every 15 years, something mysterious happens. They then slaughter nearly all their pigs, and after a huge party, they go to war against their neighbours. This, they claim, is something they do out of deference to their ancestors. Rappaport's explanation is never the less different. He shows that when the pig population increases, the Tsembaga run into problems keeping the pigs under control. The pigs destroy crops, and the cost of looking after them becomes prohibitive. At the same time, the soil is impoverished, as usually happens after a few years of slash-and-burn cultivation. When the pigs are slaughtered and the Tsembaga go to war, followed by building a new village in a new location, they do so for ecological reasons. They gain access to new land, and can begin raising pigs in modest numbers again.

Rappaport's explanation was not just ecological; like Harris' analysis of the sacred cows, it was also functionalist. Although the book was praised and widely read, not least by students, it was also criticised. If the local Tsembaga explanation of their sacrifice, the ritual and their ensuing displacement was incorrect, where was the decision in fact taken? Was there a 'great ecologist in the sky' who decided when they should get rid of their surplus of pigs and move on? And if ecological functionality governed the pig slaughter, why did they not kill and eat a moderate number of pigs every year instead of engaging in huge, rare and wasteful rituals? Rappaport responded to his critics in interesting and creative ways, and he modified his earlier views on several issues. The details of the debate are irrelevant here, but the 1984 edition of the book gives a good impression of the breadth of issues raised by *Pigs*.

What this kind of study may tell us is perhaps not so much how ecology affects society, but about societal flexibility in managing the relationship with its ecological surroundings. For whenever a simple ecological explanation of a complex cultural practice is offered, the critical questions which inevitably pose themselves, make one realise the variability in human responses to the environment. As my teacher Harald Eidheim once said 'Cultural ecology may not tell us a lot about ecology, but it definitely teaches us something about culture'.

NATURE AS A SOCIAL CONSTRUCTION

So far in this chapter, we have dealt with ways in which objective nature 'out there' and 'in here' is articulated with social and cultural conditions, but the fact is that anthropologists have, particularly in recent years, been much more preoccupied with nature as it is conceptualised locally. In other words, the focus here is on *nature in culture* rather than on *nature in itself*. This perspective conforms to a more general shift in anthropology, towards interpreting symbols and meaning instead of trying to account for or explain structure. Research about nature as it appears to natives concerns only to a limited extent the objective effects of nature on culture and society, and if it has a message about human nature, it is likely to be that it is malleable and contextually sensitive. Yet there are universalist ideas on offer here, too. With inspiration from Durkheim and Mauss, Lévi-Strauss has long been interested in systems of classification which categorise natural phenomena. This topic will be dealt with more fully in the next chapter, but it is none the less relevant to mention that the reason for his interest is not a wish to document the breadth of human systems of classification. Although Lévi-Strauss approaches variation from a cultural relativist perspective (cultures are unique, integrated entities), his goal is to understand the universal structures of the human mind.

Research on nature as a cultural construction is wide-ranging. A typical contribution is, perhaps, Peter Worsley's book *Knowledges* (1997), a book about different ways of relating mentally and culturally to nature, drawing on ethnography from contemporary western societies as well as Australia and Melanesia. This kind of research is often comparative; for example, some years ago, a collection of articles about different peoples' relationships to trees was published. Both ethnobotanics and ethnozoology are well established fields which reveal variations and similarities in different peoples' classification of living things. Sometimes, this research becomes politically volatile, as in Arne Kalland's studies of the whale in western cosmologies (Kalland 1993). Kalland, a Norwegian anthropologist and a supporter of (limited) whaling, argues that certain environmental organisations have developed an image of 'the super whale', a non-existent creature combining features from various whale species, which appears as a totem, a sacred animal. He thereby argues that a common view of the whale in western societies is based on religion rather than science.

Research on cultural representations of nature may become politically relevant in other ways as well, as, for example, in Edvard Hviding's detailed studies of traditional resource management in the Solomon Islands in 1996. His research has provided input for the environmental conservation work carried out by local authorities and international organisations alike, since it has shown how modern notions about sustainability may be compatible with traditional ideas about culture and nature.

If we accept that knowledge about nature, at least to some extent, is governed by cultural evaluations and categories, there is no reason to assume that scientific knowledge about nature should not be studied as a form of cultural knowledge. This would involve taking research on the influence of nature on culture and society with a pinch of salt; it is, at least to some extent, framed and informed by the notions prevalent in the researcher's own society. According to this perspective, science is itself a form of cultural specialisation on a par with others, and as such it should not be studied as either more true or more false than other forms of knowledge about nature.

Far from all anthropologists finding it fruitful to see science as a form of knowledge similar to others *tout court*; arguably, only a small minority do. Since the subject has ambitions to build scientific knowledge itself, such an attitude would at least partly undermine one's own project. However, many anthropologists see the usefulness of studying science as a cultural construction without thereby taking a position as to whether it is more or less credible than other forms of knowledge about the world. For obviously, the questions and methods of science must come from somewhere, and even if science can establish valid knowledge about nature, it is frequently relevant to investigate why it raises particular types of question rather than others.

Even if local assumptions about nature and 'naturalness' in contemporary western societies are not necessarily scientific (they are very often not), they often have a dynamic relationship with the scientific production of knowledge. Scientists are themselves inhabitants of particular societies and inevitably think through their cultural categories. In a very influential book, *After Nature*, Marilyn Strathern (1992) compares English and Melanesian ways of thinking about procreation. While many Melanesian peoples regard newly born infants as reborn ancestors/ancestresses, the English regard children as entirely new persons. In the last part of the book, Strathern argues that the new reproductive technologies – from test tubes to surrogate mothers and (in a possible near future) cloning – involve a shift in the relationship between culture and nature. When it becomes possible, to an increasing degree, to decide what kind of child one is going to have, human procreation is no longer regarded as something natural; a former part of nature becomes incorporated into culture and subjected to its control. The boundary between nature and culture is, in other words, not an absolute one.

The concept 'conservation of nature' points in the same direction. It intimates that nature is no longer capable of looking after itself, and therefore depends on the protection offered by culture to survive. This way of relating to nature is extraordinary in the history of human society. Although it is unlikely that the contrast between culture and nature exists universally (as Lévi-Strauss has claimed), nature is generally conceived of as something existing outside of culture, and often as something potentially threatening to the social order. It has accordingly been claimed that whereas farmers tend to see nature as an enemy (wild animals and unwanted plants destroy the crops etc.), hunter-gatherers regard nature as a friend because they depend on it for survival. This may be true of several cases. But that external nature should cease to exist as anything but a segment of the world that needs the active support of culture to cope, is an alien thought everywhere except, perhaps, in western society.

Much important work in this area focuses on ideology. It has become apparent that a great number of ideologies justify existing power relationships by claiming that they are 'natural', an integral part of 'the order of nature' or something similar. This is not merely the case in western society, where slavery was defended by referring to the 'natural place' of the 'Negro' as a subservient member of the species, and where anti-feminists have said similar things about women. The same kind of ideology is also widespread in traditional societies. Naturalisation is, in a word, a common ideological device which serves to reproduce existing power relations. If somebody says 'That is just the way things are', or 'You cannot change human nature', there are sound reasons to search for the subtext. What is the underlying message of such statements? In many cases, the answer is power. In many societies, myths are called upon for illustration and confirmation. For years, anthropologists and others believed that traditional societies had originally been matriarchal (governed by women) before becoming patriarchal. Detailed studies never the less showed that the stories about the 'original matriarchy' were myths related by men to justify the present order. According to these myths, there were serious flaws in the fabric of society during the period of female reign, but then the men took over, and it soon turned out that male rule was part of the natural order.

A great deal of culture, any culture, has an air of taken-for-grantedness about it. People do not reflect on the fact that whatever it is that they know, say and do is learned according to an invisible script, that most of it could have been different, and that it is definitely not natural. This implicit kind of knowledge is sometimes spoken of as *doxa*, sometimes as *tacit knowledge*. It is rarely spoken about, either because it is taken for granted, or because the agents do not even know that they possess it. We all know a lot of things that we do not even know we know. This knowledge is frequently naturalised (seen as natural) and it is the task of anthropology to unpack it and show how it enters into a particular, cultural knowledge regime.

THE IMPLICIT AND THE EMBODIED

What about the body then; there, at last, we must have identified something solidly natural? In a certain sense, the body is natural. It breathes and discards waste, it needs food and rest, and it goes through a pre-programmed process of ageing. Anthropological studies of the body have not delved into these aspects of the body, but have instead explored how the body is made cultural in ways that make it appear to be natural.

In a text which may have been half a century ahead of its time, Mauss described what he spoke of as 'the techniques of the body' (Mauss 1979 [1938]). Experience had taught him that even peoples who regarded themselves as closely related in cultural terms, used their bodies in different ways, and that body techniques often changed quickly. Mauss, who was born in 1872, had learned to swim well before the last turn of the century. He had been instructed in classic breast stroke swimming, and learned to fill his mouth with water, which he then spat out 'like a small steamboat' between the strokes. This technique, which appeared natural at the time, had been completely replaced by other styles by the 1930s. Mauss also mentions an English regiment during the First World War, who had been assigned to dig trenches, but who proved incapable of handling French spades. Thus, all spades had to be changed whenever English troops replaced French ones. Mauss also speaks about differences in marching, walking, running, coughing and spitting, eating and so on. To describe these incorporated techniques (the term incorporated stems from the Latin *in corpore*, that is in the body), he suggests the term *habitus*, which may be translated as embodied, routinised habit. Mauss remarks that not only do such techniques vary from society to society, but they also vary within a given society. Differences in body techniques within a society testify to both gender-based and class differences, and often to others as well.

Only since the 1980s have a considerable number of anthropologists become interested in the body, often inspired by Pierre Bourdieu's reintroduction of Mauss's concept of *habitus*. The body is interesting in several ways; it is both nature, culture and individuality, but of particular interest here is the fact that the embodied knowledge is implicit. Much of what we know, we know with our bodies.

The widespread tendency to exaggerate the significance of verbal communication in social and cultural research has been mentioned earlier. Since academics are, if anything, verbal people struggling to express themselves accurately and lucidly, we may tend to assume that others are similarly afflicted. But, as the foregoing discussion suggests, a great deal of human communication and behaviour is non-verbal. Sometimes one may describe these skills when told 'Hold the fork in the left hand and the knife in the right hand; eat with your mouth closed; eat silently and avoid belching'. In other cases, one can only describe a particular skill through demonstration: How does one cycle or swim? Yet other kinds of knowledge are, as mentioned above, of such a character that the informants are unaware of even possessing them. Faced with such cultural skills and notions, anthropologists have a demanding task in identifying and accounting for, not only the *tacit knowledge*, but also the *embodied knowledge*. The English soldiers mentioned by Mauss would never have reflected on the fact that they had learned to dig in a culturally specific way with culturally specific spades, had they not been asked, due to circumstances, to dig with French spades.

Culture is not a thing. It has no surface, boundaries or mass. It cannot be observed, touched and squeezed. It is like an invisible lump of slime, it flows, varies, overlaps, changes. It is both explicit and implicit, verbal and embodied. The present author and the readers presumably share a cultural idiom since we assign roughly the same meaning to this sentence. But closer acquaintance would quickly reveal that we have 'different cultures' in a lot of areas. Perhaps we hold different beliefs regarding the afterlife, different views about child raising and the good life, and perhaps indeed we dig holes in the ground in fundamentally different ways. It is in the span between whatever is shared, whether explicit or implicit, and whatever varies, that research on culture has its proper place. Neither insisting that all individuals are different from each other nor claims to the effect that all x'es think alike, can offer descriptions which are satisfactory at the end of the day. For this reason it is important to express oneself accurately, whether the concept of culture is retained or rejected. When speaking of differences, does one refer to gender roles, swimming techniques, linguistic understanding or food habits? Does a particular generalisation apply to all x'es or only to some of them? If cultural communities are a worthy subject of study, and they are, it is in other words necessary to regard them as shifting, overlapping entities. Whatever it is that the reader has in common with a contemporary from the same town is not identical to whatever it is that he or she shares with the neighbour, but both forms of sharing are important and cultural in the sense of being learned and common to a group of persons.

Thirty years of intense debate over the concept of culture has taught us at least one lesson, namely how crucial it is to be cautious and accurate whenever using the term culture, and to have one's guard up whenever someone else does it.

SOCIOBIOLOGY

A theoretical orientation which has received much attention in recent years is one which traces its historical origins, not to Marx, Durkheim or Weber, but to Darwin. This school of thought has been discussed briefly in a couple of places already; we now take a slightly more thorough look at it. It may be prudent to begin by stating that virtually no educated western person doubts that humans are products of evolution, and that we are close relatives of the great apes. There are no serious alternatives to Darwin's theory of evolution through natural selection – notwithstanding certain ambitious attempts motivated by religious faith – although there is considerable disagreement among scholars regarding both the interpretation of the theory and the scope of its explanatory power. For example, many biologists hold that there are plenty of natural phenomena which cannot be explained through the Darwinist principle of natural selection. The question which is relevant in the present context, is what Darwinism can tell us about the social and cultural lives of humans.

Popular science and mass media sometimes appear to suggest that natural science will sooner or later offer answers to all meaningful questions concerning what it is to be human. For example, they may announce that 'finally, scientists have found the gene for homosexuality', that the human DNA sequence is 'the book of life' and that it has been scientifically proven that men have an inborn tendency to be more promiscuous than women. If one looks carefully at the research underlying such generalisations, one is quickly brought to the conclusion that it is necessary to approach them with a sober and sceptical frame of mind. Not only is there deep disagreement as to the adequate interpretation of scientific findings, but there is also disagreement as to what is to be counted as scientific findings, that is to say the *validity* of a particular set of results. This does not mean that it is impossible to establish valid knowledge, but that it is much more difficult to conclude unequivocally about whatever it is that takes place in the spiritual lives of humans than what happens when an amoeba is divided in two.

Human sociobiology, that is the study of humans in society regarded as a biological species, was a discipline which, in spite of its obvious predecessors, was established in the 1960s and 1970s. A high point in its history was the publication, in 1975, of Edward O Wilson's book *Sociobiology*. Wilson regarded the social sciences as immature disciplines which ought to be 're-integrated' into the mother science, biology. Anthropologists did not take gently to the provocation, and many voiced their disbelief and rage at such a preposterous proposal. Sahlins quickly wrote the pamphlet *The Use and Abuse of Biology* (1977), which showed what the conflict consisted in. First of all, Wilson knew little about existing research on cultural variation, and second, he disregarded the ability of humans to create order and to act self-consciously on the basis of perceptions and notions of their own making. Wilson saw biological adaptation where Sahlins saw cultural creativity and autonomy.

Later, particularly since the beginning of the 1990s, the Darwinian research on culture and society has become more sophisticated than the early efforts from Wilson and others. Its defenders now admit that culture is not always adaptive (that is, biologically functional), and they accept that human actions cannot be understood as pure adaptation. An important branch of sociobiology now labels itself evolutionary psychology, thereby indicating something of a fresh start. Whereas Wilson and his generation were especially interested in sex and violence as the constitutive activities of humanity, contemporary research is preoccupied with the study of human mental faculties. If it is correct, as most scholars assume, that modern humans appeared around 200,000 years ago in Africa, and that they had evolved through natural selection, which traits characterising contemporary human beings can then be understood as outcomes of this process of selection? (Some of these researchers take this postulated connection quite far, and claim, for example, that humans have an innate propensity to prefer paintings which contain green fields and quiet water. Others are more moderate in their claims.) The research aims to establish valid generalisations about the human mind as it has evolved biologically.

Much can be said about the new Darwinist social science, but at least it cannot be said to be racist. Evolutionary psychologists are more struck by the similarities than by the differences between cultural groups, unlike most anthropologists. To evolutionary psychologists, the variations in intelligence and other innate properties that they study, exist within every population, not between them. A supporter of a version of this view, the acclaimed science populariser Jared Diamond, writes in the introduction to one of his books (Diamond 1992) that the most intelligent people he has ever met were tribals in the New Guinean highlands. He explains this by pointing out that they lack those crutches for thought that writing and other forms of information technology represent in our society, and that they must therefore be intellectually alert continuously; they must remember everything they need to know, he claims, and besides, they live risky and dangerous lives and are forced to concentrate mentally much of the time. Of course, his general description is highly debatable, but it can serve as a reminder that the new sociobiology – whether or not it calls itself evolutionary psychology – takes deep cultural variations into account (which the old sociobiology did not) and takes the mental unity of humanity as a starting point.

Most anthropologists are unenthusiastic about evolutionary psychology. They regard its generalisations as superficial and its explanations as misleading. If humans at least to a certain degree are self-defining creatures, our innate properties have minimal explanatory value when we try to understand cultural variation. Indeed, the late Marvin Harris, who was a materialist and a believer in positivist methods, and therefore might have been a natural ally for the new Darwinists, sharply criticised it on such a basis. Since the cultural variation existing in the world is much greater than the genetic variation, Harris (1998) stated that we need other explanations than the sociobiological ones in order to understand culture.

In my personal view, there are many exciting possibilities for cooperation between social and cultural anthropologists on the one hand, and scholars with a biological perspective on the other, but these opportunities are regularly lost in aggressive academic turf wars and a failure to take each other seriously as representatives of genuine knowledge, even if based on different foundations. The sociobiologists and their successors look at life through a pair of binoculars, with the gaze fixed on the minute hand. (The hour hand and telescope are reserved for the palaeontologists and geologists.) Social and cultural anthropologists regard life through a magnifying glass, concentrating on the second hand. They also ask different kinds of questions to their respective materials. Sociobiologists ask, 'What is a human being?', responding perfectly credibly that the human species is a little twig at the end of a branch on the great tree of life. The social and cultural anthropologists ask, 'What does it mean to be a human', and come up with a totally different set of answers (Ingold 1994). The sociobiologists are interested in understanding similarities, while social and cultural anthropologists are, with a few exceptions, still obsessed with difference.

If we can reconcile ourselves to these differences, accepting that both kinds of approaches are necessary, it will in the future be easier both to ignore each other when appropriate, to define the boundaries of the respective forms of knowledge, and to cooperate when the situation allows it. At the time of writing, few signs of such an ecumenical attitude are visible in the intellectual landscape.

FURTHER READING

Diamond, Jared (1992) *The Third Chimpanzee: The Evolution and Future of the Human Animal*. New York: HarperCollins.
Howell, Signe and Roy Willis, eds. (1989) *Societies at Peace*. London: Routledge.

8
Thought

It has already been mentioned that anthropology is concerned with that which takes place between people, not with their innermost feelings and thoughts. How can it then be that this chapter is going to be about thought? The answer is not simple. It may justly be said that thought has an important social aspect; in different societies, the inhabitants think differently because of differences in the circumstances of learning, different experiences, etc. At the same time, thought has an undeniable private and personal dimension, which cannot be studied directly with the methods available to anthropologists.

Fortunately, thoughts are usually expressed in social life, for example when people say what they think or express it through their acts, in rituals and other public performances. Therefore, thought can be explored, if often obliquely, through the field methods available to anthropology; participant observation, questions and answers, and common curiosity.

THE RATIONALITY DEBATE

Studies of thought and modes of reasoning have been central in the history of anthropology from the nineteenth century to the present day. The most famous (and possibly most voluminous) anthropological work from the years before the fieldwork revolution was James Frazer's twelve-volume *The Golden Bough* (1890/1912), a comparative work about myth, religion and cosmologies among virtually all the peoples the author had heard about. Frazer shared the evolutionist views of his contemporaries and had little faith in the ability of 'savages' to think logically and rationally. A younger contemporary of Frazer, the philosopher Lucien Lévy-Bruhl, was less impressive in his use of empirical materials, but to compensate, he was more analytically lucid than Frazer. Lévy-Bruhl described traditional peoples as representatives of what he described, in an unfortunate turn of phrase, as a 'pre-logical mode of thought'. However, Lévy-Bruhl emphasised that the term 'pre-logical' did not necessarily refer to a developmental or evolutionary line of progress, but rather that the unhampered, metaphorical and symbol-laden way of thinking he associated with traditional peoples was more fundamental, and logically prior to, logical thought. Contemporary moderns may have retained their ability to think in a 'pre-logical' way, but a logical rationality has been superimposed on it, as it were.

Lévy-Bruhl was criticised sharply by several of his contemporaries, who pointed out that the empirical foundation for his lofty generalisations was weak to say the least. However, it would none the less be Lévy-Bruhl's books from the years around the First World War that set the stage for one of the most exciting theoretical debates in anthropology, where contributors from several academic fields discussed (and still do) to what degree there are fundamental differences in thought styles between peoples, and conversely, to what extent it may be said that a common human rationality exists.

One of the first to criticise Lévy-Bruhl on an empirical basis was Evans-Pritchard. In the 1930s, he had several lengthy periods of fieldwork in the Sudan. His Nuer research has already been mentioned, but his 1937 book about the Azande is no less important (some would argue that it is much more important) than *The Nuer*. Whereas Evans-Pritchard's first Nuer monograph dealt with politics, ecology and kinship, *Witchcraft, Magic and Oracles Among the Azande* is a book about the system of knowledge and belief in a traditional people, and as such, it was one of the first of its kind. One would in fact have to wait for Kluckhohn's *Navaho Witchcraft* (1944) for another study of comparable depth.

The Azande live right in the middle of the African continent, only a few hundred kilometres south of the Nuer; but in terms of culture and social organisation, they are very different from the nomadic peoples to the north. They are sedentary crop growers, politically relatively centralised with aristocratic clans and princes. At the time of Evans-Pritchard's research, they had been incorporated into the British empire, and the power of the traditional rulers had been reduced considerably.

The Zande belief in witchcraft, and their use of various remedies to control it, are well documented in Evans-Pritchard's book. Witchcraft, as it is defined in anthropology, is distinguished from magic in that it is an invisible force. Accordingly, it is difficult to decide who is responsible when someone is struck by witchcraft. Magic is, on the contrary, the result of rites and technologies which are known, and one may consult recognised magicians for assistance with one's problems. In societies where witchcraft is assumed to exist, it is thus necessary to develop methods to expose the witches. When a Zande experiences a 'mishap' (Evans-Pritchard's term), he is likely to blame witchcraft for it, and he may begin to suspect people he believes have a reason to want to harm him. (It stands to reason that like other peoples who are concerned with witchcraft, the Azande may be said to fit Benedict's 'paranoid' cultural type fairly well.)

If a Zande walks on the forest path, stumbles and hurts himself, only to discover that the wound won't heal, he blames witchcraft. If one objects that occasional stumbling is normal, he might respond that yes, it is normal, but I walk this path every day and have never stumbled before, and besides, wounds normally begin to heal after a few days. When a group of Azande sit under an elevated granary on poles (to protect the cereals against wild animals), which suddenly collapses and hurts them badly, the immediate cause is that termites have slowly perforated the poles until they were no longer capable of keeping the granary stable. But the Azande will say that it was extremely unlikely that they should sit beneath their granary just as it fell, and thus witchcraft had to be involved somehow. Deaths among Azande are always caused by witchcraft, Evans-Pritchard reports; disease is usually caused by it.

The Azande have at their disposal a range of techniques enabling them to explore whether or not a suspect is actually a witch. (The term witch is, in anthropological usage, gender neutral.) Most commonly, they consult so-called oracles, that is spiritual beings who talk to them through mediums. One popular medium is a kind of sounding board, and there are others, but the most expensive and famous is the poison oracle. To make it communicate, one needs a strong plant-derived poison and a chicken. The chicken is fed the poison, and the oracle is asked whether a certain person is a witch or not. If the chicken dies, the answer is yes; if it survives, the accused is innocent.

In the old days, Evans-Pritchard says, witches were regularly executed. Under the 'indirect rule' of the British, implemented from the early twentieth century, princely power was reduced, and judicial power transferred to the colonial courts of law. Therefore, Evans-Pritchard himself never witnessed executions of witches. In his time, many believed that the very institution of witchcraft would gradually disappear thanks to 'progress'. The oracles were not infallible. When a witch died, their belly would be cut open to establish whether it contained a certain 'witchcraft substance', described as a dark lump of flesh. If a witch had been convicted and killed, and no such substance subsequently found, the relatives of the dead person could demand compensation.

Evans-Pritchard describes the witchcraft institution in a sober and morally neutral way, skilfully showing how the Azande think and act rationally and logically, given their cultural context. If one were to ask an educated Zande if it might not be the case that bacteria, not witchcraft, made him ill, he might respond that yes, of course, but this so-called explanation said nothing about the reason for *his* illness right *now*; the bacteria were around continuously, so why wasn't his neighbour ill, and why didn't the illness occur last year? The logic is, as we see, impeccable. Unlike medical science, the witchcraft institution offers answers to the pressing questions 'Why me?' and 'Why now?'

The book on witchcraft is a remarkable read, and it has rightly been praised as one of the few books that set an agenda for research and discussion which lasted more than half a century after its publication. The book offers rare, deep insights into the knowledge system of a traditional people, and shows how it is coherent, gives meaning to the world, and explains unusual events. Had Evans-Pritchard been ideologically bolder, he might have compared the institution of witchcraft with religions such as Christianity. The book also shows how the witchcraft institution is functional in the sense that is socially integrative. Usually, the people accused of witchcraft belonged to politically weak lineages (nobody would dream of accusing a prince), and he points out that the institution functioned as a security valve by channelling discontent and frustrations away from the social order (which would have been exceedingly difficult to change anyway) towards individuals who became scapegoats. Much of the later literature on witchcraft in Africa, especially that published in the 1950s, is purely structural-functionalist, and strongly emphasises that those who are accused of witchcraft are often women, who, in virilocal societies, are outsiders without strong local political support. Evans-Pritchard offers a richer picture, supplementing the functional analysis with a vivid description of local life-worlds.

Unfortunately, many of those who have never read the book itself have heard about it through secondary sources, and therefore believe that it is a condescending, functionalistic description of a primitive people who believe in phenomena that do not exist. The main culprit in creating this distorted view of the book is the philosopher Peter Winch. In 1958, he published the very challenging book *The Idea of a Social Science and Its Relation to Philosophy*, where Evans-Pritchard appears as one of his main opponents. Winch refers to a number of intermittent remarks in the Azande book, where the anthropologist expresses the view that witches obviously do not exist. In an appendix to the book, Evans-Pritchard distinguishes between three kinds of knowledge: mystical knowledge based on the belief in invisible and unverifiable forces; commonsensical knowledge based on everyday experience; and scientific knowledge based on the tenets of logic and the experimental method. The middle, quantitatively largest category is common to Azande and Englishmen; the latter exists only in modern societies, whereas the first category is typical of societies where one believes in witchcraft. Winch argues that the two systems of knowledge – the English one and that of the Azande – cannot be ranked in this way; they can in fact not be ranked at all. All knowledge is socially produced, he continues; and mentions the widespread 'superstitious' belief in meteorology as a modern equivalent to Zande witchcraft beliefs. In other words, Winch regards scientific knowledge as a kind of culturally produced knowledge on a par with other forms of knowledge.

The criticism of Evans-Pritchard is not based on fabricated evidence, but as I have shown, it does not do justice to his pioneering, and largely non-judgemental exposition of a non-western knowledge system. Be this as it may, Winch's book gave the impetus to a broad debate about rationality and relativism. It would give the initial inspiration for several books, dissertations and conferences in the 1960s and later. Anthropologists, sociologists and philosophers contributed.

The criticism against Evans-Pritchard contains several independent questions, at least three. The first and second concern methodological possibilities and limitations. The third concerns the nature of knowledge and is anthropological in a philosophical sense. First: Is it possible to translate from one system of knowledge to another without distorting it by introducing concepts initially alien to that 'other' world of representations? Second: Does a context-independent or neutral language exist to describe systems of knowledge? Third: Do all humans reason in fundamentally the same way? There are, perhaps, no final answers to any of these questions, and yet (or perhaps therefore) they remain important. We should keep in mind here that Evans-Pritchard himself criticised Lévy-Bruhl's dichotomy between logical and pre-logical thought, and emphasised time and again that the Azande were just as rational as westerners, but that they reasoned logically and rationally from premises which were, at the end of the day, erroneous when it came to witchcraft. Winch's question was whether general, unquestionable criteria exist to evaluate the premises or axioms, and he replies that this is not the case, since the axioms themselves are socially created and therefore not true in an absolute, ahistorical sense.

It should be noted here that a research area which has grown rapidly since the 1980s is the so-called STS field, that is the sociological study of technology and science. In this research, western science and technology are studied as cultural products, and most of its practitioners adhere to the so-called symmetry principle, which entails that the same terminology and the same methods of analysis should be used for failures as for successes; in other words, that what we are doing is looking at science as a social fact, not as truth or falsity. Similarly, most anthropologists would argue that our task consists of making sense of 'the others', not judging whether they are right or wrong.

CLASSIFICATION AND POLLUTION

Unfortunately, it is necessary to leave the fascinating controversies about rationality and the rich anthropological research tradition dealing with witchcraft here. Another, no less interesting, way of approaching other knowledges and thought systems, points the searchlight towards classification. All peoples are aware that different things and persons exist in the world, but they subdivide them in different, locally defined ways.

In 1903, Durkheim and Mauss published a book about primitive classification, which was to a great extent based on ethnography from Australia. They argued that there existed a connection between the classification of natural phenomena and social order. This connection has been explored by later generations of scholars, but historically, there has been a difference here between European social anthropology and North American cultural anthropology. The latter tradition is generally less sociologically oriented than the former, and often explores symbolic systems as autonomous entities, without connecting them systematically to social conditions. Geertz once wrote that whereas society was integrated in a 'causal-functional way', culture was integrated in a 'logico-meaningful way', and could thus be studied independently of the social. In social anthropology (and, in all fairness, to many American anthropologists), such a delineation is unsatisfactory, since a main preoccupation in this tradition consists of understanding symbolic worlds through their relation to social organisation. Power, politics and technology inevitably interact with knowledge production in a society.

Of the many books about classification and society that have been published since Durkheim and Mauss, two have been especially influential. Researchers and students continue to return to them, and although both were initially published in the 1960s, they do not appear dated even today.

Mary Douglas studied under Evans-Pritchard, and carried out fieldwork among the Lele in Kasai (southern Congo, then Belgian Congo) in the 1950s. She published a monograph about the Lele, but she is far better known for her later theoretical contributions. *Purity and Danger* (1966), in particular, has exerted an almost unparalleled influence on anthropological research dealing with thought and social life. In this book, Douglas combines influences from her native British structural functionalism and French structuralism, which she became familiar with early on, partly due to her fieldwork in a part of Africa where most of the researchers were French. The main argument is inspired by Durkheim and Mauss, and states that classification of nature and the body reflects society's ideology about itself. However, her main interest was in accounting for *pollution*, classificatory impurities and their results, and one of the central chapters of the book is devoted to a discussion of food prohibitions in the Old Testament. Animals which do not 'fit in' are deemed unfit for human consumption, and include, among others, maritime animals without fins and, famously, the pig. The pig has cloven hoofs but does not chew the cud, and there is no category available for this kind of animal. This is what makes it polluting.

Douglas' theory is as far removed as possible from Marvin Harris' interpretation of sacred cows, and indeed, Harris has argued that the impurity of the pig in western Asia is caused by objective factors, notably the disease-inducing germs which can be present in badly cooked pork. Douglas' views on this kind of explanation are of the same kind as Lévi-Strauss' views on Malinowski. According to Lévi-Strauss, the practically oriented Malinowski saw culture as nothing more than 'a gigantic metaphor for the digestive system'. The connection between the order of society and the order of classificatory systems is crucial to Douglas' theory. Among other things, she refers to holy men and women in Hinduism and Christianity, who invert dominant perceptions of pure and impure in order to highlight the otherworldly character of their lives. She mentions a Christian saint who is said to have drunk puss from an infected wound since personal cleanliness is incompatible with the status of the holy woman; and Indian *sudhus* are famous for their transgressive practices, such as drinking from human skulls, eating rotten food, sleeping on spiked mats and so on.

Phenomena that do not fit in, *anomalies*, must be taken care of ideologically lest they pollute the entire classificatory system. If this is not done efficiently, they threaten the order of society. There has to be order in nature, just as there is order in society. Douglas' most famous anomaly is taken from her Lele ethnography, namely the African pangolin. This forest animal is a mammal, but it has scales like a fish and gives birth to only one or two offspring, just like a human. The Lele have circumscribed the pangolin with a great number of rules and prohibitions to keep it under control; it can be eaten, but only under very special circumstances, and one is usually well advised to avoid close contact with it. A subgroup of anomalies are the phenomena known as *matter out of place*, that is objects, actions or ideas which appear in the 'wrong' context. The typical example is a human hair, usually far from unaesthetic when it grows out of a head, but repulsive if it floats in a bowl of soup.

Douglas does not write about humour, but one must be allowed to point out that virtually everything that is funny belongs to the same category as the hair floating in the soup; jokes nearly always derive their punchline from wrong contextualisation. Perhaps that is why Geertz once wrote that understanding a different culture is like understanding a joke. When one is able to laugh at the natives' jokes, one has internalised local norms about correct and incorrect contextualisation. This indicates that one has understood a great deal.

Douglas has been criticised for placing too much emphasis on integration in her analyses. Just as Geertz' concept of culture seems to presuppose that all the pieces of the jigsaw puzzle of culture fall perfectly into place, Douglas assumes that both society and knowledge systems are ordered and fit together. One should not rule out the possibility that she may be right. Classificatory systems change – there are many secularised Jews and Muslims who eat pork – and there is clearly a greater variation and more direct contestation, especially in complex societies, than Douglas is prepared to admit. But this very variation also seems to confirm the validity of Douglas' model. When university educated northern European Marxist-Leninists took manual jobs in the 1970s, loyal to the principle of self-proletarianisation, they turned dominant classifications on their head in their attempt to change the very ideological foundations of society. In a racially segregated society such as the American South, few actions are more radical, both politically and in terms of classification, than to marry across the colour line. Both these examples show that conscious transgressions serve to confirm the essential validity of the dominant mode of classification.

Douglas' ideas about matter out of place, anomalies, pollution and the analogies between the body, nature and society, have been exceptionally productive. The next chapter will briefly indicate how some of these ideas may be transposed to studies of multi-ethnic societies, just to illustrate their fruitfulness.

THE SAVAGE MIND

The other indispensable book about classification and society is Lévi-Strauss's masterpiece *La pensée sauvage* (1962, *The Savage Mind*, 1966). Like Douglas, Lévi-Strauss is inspired by Durkheim and Mauss, but he also wishes to disprove Lévy-Bruhl's ideas about 'pre-logical thought' once and for all. However, even in the first chapter, it becomes apparent that Lévi-Strauss is closer to his predecessor than one might have expected.

The main topic of *The Savage Mind* is totemism. This enigmatic phenomenon has been the subject of much anthropological theory and speculation for more than 100 years. Totemism may be defined as a form of classification whereby individuals or groups (which may be clans) have a special, often mythically based relationship to certain aspects of nature, usually animals or plants, but it could also be, for example, mountain formations or events like thunderstorms. Groups or persons have certain commitments towards their totem; it may be forbidden to eat it, the totem may give protection, in many cases the groups are named after their totem, and sometimes they identify with it (members of the eagle clan are brave and have a lofty character). In traditional societies, totemism is especially widespread in the Americas, in Oceania and Africa. A great number of competing interpretations of totemism had been proposed before Lévi-Strauss. The Scottish lawyer MacLennan, the first to develop a theory of totemism (in 1869), saw it simply as a form of primitive religion, but it later became more common to see it in a more utilitarian light; totemic animals and plants were respected because they were economically useful. This was Malinowski's view.

Departing radically from such views, Lévi-Strauss developed a theory of totemism seeing it as a form of classification encompassing both natural and social dimensions, thereby defining it as part of the knowledge system of a society, and far from being a functional result of some economic adaptation. Lévi-Strauss claims indebtedness to Radcliffe-Brown, but in fact, his theory was entirely original. Totemic animals are respected not because they are good to eat, but because they are *good to think (bons à penser)*. The natural series of totems at the disposal of a tribe is related to the social series of clans or other internal groupings in such a way that the relationships between the totems correspond metaphorically to the relationships between the social groups. Totemism thereby bridges the gap between nature and culture, deepening the knowledge about both in the process.

'The savage mind', or undomesticated thinking (which might have been a better English title), is thus not there in order to be useful or functional (or even aesthetically pleasing), but in order to be thought. In the chapter 'The science of the concrete', which introduces the topic of the book, this is made clear. Here, Lévi-Strauss develops his famous distinction between *le bricoleur* and *l'ingenieur*, between *bricolage* (associational, nonlinear thought) and 'engineering' (logical thinking) as two styles of thought which he links with traditional and modern societies, respectively. Unlike what many had argued before, including Lévy-Bruhl, there was no qualitative difference between 'primitive' and 'modern' thought. The difference consisted in the raw material they had at their disposal. While the modern 'engineer' builds abstractions upon abstractions (writing, numbers, geometrical drawings), the traditional 'bricoleur' creates abstractions with the aid of physical objects he is able to observe directly (animals, plants, rocks, rivers, etc.). Whereas the modern person has become dependent on writing as a 'crutch for thought', his opposite number in a traditional society uses whatever is at hand for cognitive assistance. The French word *bricoleur* can be translated as a jack-of-all-trades, an imaginative improviser who creates new objects by combining old ones which happen to be close at hand. In order to illustrate the contrast between the two thought styles, Lévi-Strauss speaks of music and poetry as modern cultural phenomena where 'the undomesticated' property of the mind can still be glimpsed.

Although the book is introduced with an apparently sharp contrast between 'us' and 'them', and although cultural difference is discussed in every subsequent chapter, the aim of *The Savage Mind* is to show that humans think alike everywhere, even if their thoughts are expressed differently. Science, which, unlike 'the science of the concrete', distinguishes sharply between the perceptible (*le sensible*) and that which can be understood in abstract terms (*l'intelligible*), thus becomes a special case of something much more general, namely undomesticated thought. But it then also becomes clear that the distance between Lévi-Strauss and Lévy-Bruhl is much less than usually assumed. Like his famous successor, Lévy-Bruhl also sees pre-logical thought as the most fundamental style of thought, and logical thought as an embellishment or a special case.

THOUGHT AND TECHNOLOGY

The cultural historian Lewis Mumford once remarked that the most authoritarian, efficient and socially repressive invention man had ever created was neither the steam engine nor the cannon, but the clock. What he had in mind were the social dimensions of the clock; it synchronises, standardises and integrates people wherever clocks exist and are respected. Right or wrong, Mumford's observation indicates the potential of technology in shaping and directing human thought and action, given the right social and cultural context. (Clocks may, naturally, be regarded as fancy jewellery in societies where there is no perceived need for synchronisation.)

Let us take a closer look at the clock. It is sometimes said that clocks were initially introduced in Europe as an aid for medieval monks who found it difficult to keep prayer times when they worked in the fields. This version of clock history is half-way between a certain degree of credibility and invention. Different kinds of timepieces had existed well before medieval monasteries, and the abbey clocks did not just regulate prayer times, but also working hours; not unlike contemporary clocks, in other words. However, it is easy to see that the clocks quickly had interesting, unintended side-effects when they became common in European towns. They were instrumental in making punctuality a virtue. They encouraged efficiency since activities could now be planned and synchronised in ways formerly unthinkable. Eventually, the clocks became indispensable for town-dwellers; they needed to 'keep time' to get to the concert house or theatre in time, to keep appointments and, increasingly, in working life. Something which has in recent years received wide attention thanks to Dava Sobel's bestselling book *Longitude*, is the fact that the accurate partitioning of the globe according to longitude was made possible only after the invention of a mechanical clock with minimal error margins. Combined with the western calendar, the clock served to dissect time into abstract entities and to establish a *linear perception of time*. This refers to a kind of time which can be conceptualised as a line where any segment of the same kind (a year, a month, an hour, etc.) is identical to any other segment, no matter when it unfolds. Clock and calendar time may be called *abstract time* since they contrast with the *concrete time* dominating most societies which are not subjected to clocks and calendars. In a temporal regime based on concrete time, time is measured as a combination of experienced, personal time, external events and societal rhythms such as day/night, harvest times and so on. A time segment such as an hour may accordingly vary in length.

Clock time is an *externalised* kind of time; it exists independently of events taking place in it, in the same way as a thermometer measures temperature irrespective of the subjective experience of heat or coldness, and quantified distance measures distance without taking subjective experience of distance into account. A kilometer is a kilometer (and about 0.62 miles) anywhere, any time. Even if everybody knows that five minutes may be both a mere instant and a lengthy period (say, in the dentist's office), and that 20°C may be warm if one enters the house on a winter's day, but cold if one sits naked in a chair after taking a shower, it is generally accepted in western societies that the quantitative measurements of such phenomena are 'truer' than the subjective experience. Such standardising ideas are alien to traditional societies, and are part and parcel of modernity, which is also built around institutions such as social planning, beliefs in progress, population statistics and a zealous drive to control nature. Typically time, which in traditional societies may not be something one *possesses* but rather something one *lives in*, is a scarce resource in contemporary, modern societies. It has been reified to such a degree that a historical preoccupation of the labour movement has been the struggle for shorter working hours, and in the late 1990s, social movements appeared which promote both 'slow cities', 'slow food' and, simply, 'slow time'.

The technological change which has been most intensively studied with a view to its relation to thought, is the introduction of writing. Lévi-Strauss hardly mentions it explicitly, but an underlying idea in his contrast between the bricoleur and the ingenieur is quite clearly that of writing versus non-writing. Jack Goody, especially in his *The Domestication of the Savage Mind* (1977), has argued that if one wants to come to grips with the kind of cognitive contrast Lévi-Strauss talks about, one must study transitions to literacy and differences between literate and non-literate societies. Among other things, Goody claims that scientific analysis and systematic, critical thought are impossible without writing. His theory about the transition to literacy as a gigantic watershed in cultural history is contested, and Goody has modified it several times himself. What everybody seems to agree about is that writing is indispensable for the cumulative growth of knowledge, and that it makes it possible to separate the utterance from the context of uttering.

Some of the criticisms of Goody have been exaggerated. Although there are many exceptions and many interesting 'intermediate forms' (societies with limited literacy in one way or another), and although local realities vary much more than a general theory is able to predict, writing does by and large make a considerable difference regarding thought styles. The Greek miracle, that is the transition from mythical to philosophical thinking in the eastern part of the Mediterranean (paralleled by similar developments in India and China), must have been linked with the development of alphabetic writing, although it was hardly the sole cause. Although the ancient philosophers were deeply interested in rhetoric, that is oral eloquence, they criticised each other's writings and revealed logical faults in each other's arguments, often with a time lag of a generation or more. Writing does not necessarily make people more 'intelligent' (a difficult concept); it is a crutch for thought which makes the continuous exercise of memory unnecessary; it externalises thoughts, and thus makes it easier to place them outside the brain. When one writes, moreover, one is likely to think along other patterns than when communicating orally, a tendency explored by the philosopher Jacques Derrida and many others. Although there are many similarities between written history based on archives and myths, there are also differences to do with falsifiability, dating and imposition of causal sequences.

Literacy is often accompanied by numeracy. The Phoenicians, maritime merchants from the ancient world, were famous book-keepers. The implications of accurate book-keeping for trade, business and forms of reciprocity in general, should not be underestimated. Technology has both social and cognitive implications here as well, even if it is necessary to explore local conditions and variations to get a full picture. Modern computers enable us to make calculations of dizzying complexity at astonishing speed; some of the readers may think they have a reasonable notion of 1 billion; but consider the fact that each well-nourished, healthy life lasts on average 2.2 billion seconds. At the same time, calculators and computers may well make us incapable of carrying out even simple calculations without their aid. The calculator has doubtless affected the ability of schoolchildren to learn double digit multiplication by rote, and digitalised pricing means that cashiers in supermarkets no longer know the prices of all the items in the shop by heart. Thermometers, books, calculators and similar devices create abstract standards and lead to both externalisation and standardisation of certain forms of knowledge.

In practice there is no question of an either-or. It is often said that humans are incapable of counting further than four without the aid of devices such as written numbers, pebbles or the like. However, we are familiar with a great number of traditional peoples, for example in Melanesia, who can count accurately and far by counting not only their toes and fingers, but other bodily parts as well. Some might get to 70 and further without using a single aid external to the body. There is, in a word, no sharp distinction between the peoples who have only their own memory at their disposal and those who are able to externalise their thoughts on paper; there are many kinds of mnemotechnical aids, and although letters and numbers may be the most consequential ones, they are not the only ones.

This brings me to a related but much less theorised field, namely music. The enormous complexity characterising Beethoven's and Mahler's symphonies would have been impossible, had the composers not lived in a society which for centuries had developed an accurate system of writing music, that is notation. Harmony is much rarer in societies without notes than in societies with them. And if one is able to read music, one can play music never heard. The parallel to writing and numbers is obvious; the statement is externalised and frozen, separated from the person who originated it. It can be appreciated in an unchanged manner anywhere and any time.

Let me finally mention a phenomenon which will be discussed from a different point of view in the next chapter. Nationalism would have been impossible without writing. In one of the most widely quoted books about the growth of national identities, Benedict Anderson (1983) shows that printing was a crucial condition for the emergence of nationalist thought and national identification. Before the advent of printing, books were expensive and rarely seen in private homes. In Europe, most books were written in Latin. When books gradually became cheaper in the second half of the fifteenth century, new markets for books, aimed at new audiences, quickly materialised: travel writing became popular, likewise novels, essays and popular science. Since profits were important to the printers (who were often also publishers), the books were increasingly published in vernacular languages. Thereby the national languages were standardised, and people living in Hamburg could read, verbatim, the same texts as people in Munich. The broad standardisation of culture represented in nationalism would not have been possible without a modern mass medium such as the printed book (and, later, the newspaper). Thus it may be said that writing has not only influenced thought about the world, but also thought about who we are. It has made it technologically possible to imagine that one belongs to the same people as millions of other persons whom one will never meet.

FURTHER READING

Douglas, Mary (1966) *Purity and Danger*. London: Routledge and Kegan Paul.

Goody, Jack (1977) *The Domestication of the Savage Mind*. Cambridge: Cambridge University Press 1977.

Lévi-Strauss, Claude (1966 [1962]) *The Savage Mind*. Chicago: University of Chicago Press.

9

Identification

No other part of anthropology receives more interest from the wider public sphere than those specialisations that are concerned with identity, or *identification*, to use a more accurate term; since we are, after all, dealing with a continuous process, not a thing people either possess or don't. Interest in cultural identity, nationhood, cultural change, identity politics and ethnicity has grown tremendously worldwide in the last few decades. Topics such as multiculturalism, politicised religion, cultural hybridity, affirmative action, culture and human rights, national self-determination and the plight of indigenous peoples have become major preoccupations in almost every country in the world; politically, personally and, naturally, for researchers. The role of anthropologists in this field varies from country to country, but the importance of anthropology as a research subject is undisputed when it comes to making sense of identities and group dynamics. Studies of ethnicity, nationalism, minority issues and cultural complexity have been at the forefront of much anthropological research for decades, and anthropological perspectives have exerted considerable influence elsewhere. In some countries, anthropologists are highly visible in the public sphere, where they are involved in ongoing debates about minority rights, immigrants, cultural changes and so on.

This chapter will resist the temptation to delve into current issues, and will instead show, through a few examples, some of the ways in which anthropologists have engaged with issues of identification. As compensation, it will hopefully become clear how classic studies may illuminate contemporary phenomena.

THE SOCIAL

When we speak about identification (or identity) in anthropology, we always refer to *social* identification. In the philosophy of identity, the term is used differently, and in everyday language, identity may equally well refer to the uniquely individual as to social groups. Social identification has to do with which groups a person belongs to, who he or she identifies with, how people establish and maintain invisible but socially efficient boundaries between *us* and *them*. The topic has been explored in social anthropology for 100 years, although the concept of identity became fashionable only towards the end of the 1970s. Durkheim's sociology, which so much of the professional tradition leans on, addressed group integration as one of its chief problems.

Identity has become so important in anthropology during recent decades because questions concerning identity have become important – socially, culturally and politically – in many of the societies we study. Some readers will immediately think about ethnic and nationalist politics, rights claims from minorities and religious revitalisation, but the question is even more far-ranging. Feminism and the civil rights movement in the USA were perhaps just as important social movements in their day as the new nationalistic liberation movements in the colonies after the Second World War. All these movements expressed similar concerns with identity; they defined the group as being based on a shared identity (gender, colour or place/nationality), and they insisted that the meaning and significance of their shared identity should be redefined. Being a woman, black or an inhabitant of a certain state should henceforth mean something different from what it had.

Of the many social identifications that may give persons living in complex societies a sense of belonging, we may briefly mention language, locality, kinship, nationality, ethnic membership, family, age, education, political views, sexual orientation, class, religion and gender as some possibilities. Of these, gender and age are the most fundamental; no society exists where gender and age are not socially significant. All these ways of identifying may give a secure sense of belonging to a group. In some societies, like segmentary lineage societies, the different segments of the clan become important; in a city, the local neighbourhood may be the main site of community feeling; and to some, professional identity may actually be more important than national identity. It is easy to see that some hard conceptual work is needed to get this seeming chaos of criss-crossing identifications in order.

CULTURE AND IDENTIFICATION

It was towards the end of the 1960s that ethnic identification seriously entered anthropology. It was the result of many disparate strands of work, but the most influential input arguably came from Fredrik Barth and his collaborators. In 1969, Barth edited *Ethnic Groups and Boundaries*, with contributions from a handful of Scandinavian anthropologists, based on a theoretical perspective which strongly contributed to a lasting change in the dominant approach to ethnic identity. Before then, it had been common to take people's group identities for granted. One was an x or a y because one had a particular culture and belonged to a particular social group, and that was all one needed to know. Barth and his collaborators presented a more dynamic model of ethnicity, where it was shown that the boundaries between groups were more ambiguous and less easily observed than formerly assumed.

Above all, there is no simple one-to-one relationship between culture and ethnic identity, despite what many still believe. There are ethnic groups with great internal cultural variation, and there are clear boundaries between ethnic groups whose mutual cultural differences are difficult to spot. Often, the variation within the group is greater on key indicators than the systematic differences between the groups. A recent example which shows this, is the relationship between the groups, or nationalities, which made up Yugoslavia. In the first half of the 1990s, wars raged between the three largest groups – Bosnians, Serbs and Croats – and journalists, politicians and diplomats alike described the conflicts as ethnic in nature and held that they could be explained through culture and ancient animosities. This is incorrect. The conflicts were relatively recent, and they were not caused in any way by cultural differences. In important respects, the differences between town and country were greater than between, for example, Serbs and Croats sharing the same territory. About 30 years before the Serbo-Croat war, Harald Eidheim had argued that there were minimal cultural differences between Sami and Norwegians on the sub-Arctic Finnmark coast, even if the ethnic boundaries were socially crucial. Sami and Norwegians had very little informal social contact, and they lived to a great extent segregated from each other, even if an outsider would have problems spotting the differences in their respective ways of life.

What matters in practice is not which objective cultural differences may exist between (or within) groups, but what kinds of relationships exist between the groups. However, an important part of this relationship is the *perception* of difference. At the ideological level, it may be important to maintain negative stereotypes of the others, that is standardised and pejorative notions about their way of life. Some militant feminists may hold that all men are potential rapists; militant right-wing Europeans may hold that all immigrants are either welfare parasites or religious imperialists; and on the Finnmark coast of the early 1960s, a common notion among ethnic Norwegians was that Sami were generally excessive drinkers and unclean. Identification draws its justification not so much from actual differences, as from the differences which become socially relevant because people highlight them and, even if they are wholly or partly fictitious, act as though they are real.

Although much of the present interest in identity is a typically modern concern, it is easy to find comparable identification processes in traditional societies. For example, it has been shown (by Arens 1978) that an important reason that Europeans for years believed that many African peoples were cannibals, was that their *neighbours* had told travellers that they were. As a matter of fact, cannibalism is unlikely to have existed as a cultural institution in the recent history of Africa.

RELATIONAL AND SITUATIONAL IDENTIFICATION

Identification happens both through establishing perceived similarities with others (one identifies with them), and through establishing differences to others. *Contrasts* are, in other words, important for all identification. Without the other, I cannot be myself; without the others, we cannot be us. If we accept that groups and communities are not given by nature, it is necessary to ask why it is that certain kinds of community appear and not others; why some become especially important while others do not, and why group membership seems to shift as one moves from situation to situation.

There is a simple answer to the last question. The reason that group membership shifts is that identification is *relational* and *situational*. Since it is only in relation to others that it is possible to define oneself, it follows logically that identification changes depending on who one currently has a relationship with. This aspect of identification is well described in sociological role theory, which emphasises that each and every person can be many different 'persons': father, son, colleague, jazz lover and so on. Most persons, irrespective of culture, have a privileged and multistranded relationship to their parents, which lasts until the parents die; and they may often be treated like youngsters by their ageing parents well after reaching 50. A person may thus be young in relation to her parents, old in relation to her children, a woman in relation to men, a townsperson in relation to rural people, a southerner in relation to people from the North, and an Asian in relation to Africans.

In anthropological research, the relational aspect of group identification has often been studied through examining social situations. If one wants to find out about a person's group memberships, one must follow them through a plethora of situations where they enter into contact with others. One will then gradually obtain a picture, or a model, of the groups the person belongs to and their relative importance for him or her.

It is often unclear in a given situation which relationship should be regarded as the most relevant one. Suppose a male anthropologist employed by a Spanish university has a supervision meeting with a female, Lebanese MA student who writes a thesis about group conflicts in the Middle East. Of course, their relationship is primarily defined as a teacher–student one, but it is very unlikely that the student's nationality, ethnic or religious origin, gender and topical specialisation would not also affect the relationship. Professional women in western societies often complain that they are being treated more like women than like colleagues, in other words that their gender identity is given primacy in situations when they themselves deem it irrelevant. In such cases, there may be *negotiations over the definition of the situation*, where the parties at the outset have definitions of each other which match badly. At a Nordic conference on identity issues some years ago, a sociologist working in Sweden, but who was born in Pakistan, asked the others in the room 'What do you perceive me as? A Pakistani, an immigrant, an immigrant sociologist or simply a sociologist?' Quite clearly, if it had been up to him, he would simply have been perceived as a sociologist. But it was not up to him. Identification is created both from the inside and the outside, in the meeting between one's own presentation of self and the perceptions of others.

IMPERATIVE AND CHOSEN IDENTITY

An often mentioned paradox in Barth's influential model of ethnicity is that he argues that ethnic identity is *both* imperative and situational. This would entail that it is both enforced and chosen, which seems logically impossible. However, it is easy to respond to the objection. Ethnic identity is imperative in the sense that one can rarely rid oneself of it entirely; if you are a Nuer, a Trobriander, a Sikh or an Englishman, you always will be. In principle, I might decide that as from tomorrow morning I shall never again utter a word in any other language than German, but I cannot prevent Norwegian from being my first language, and I cannot prevent many of my fellow humans from perceiving me as a Norwegian for the rest of my life. What is possible, however, is to negotiate strategically over definitions of situations, and to choose the situations one enters into carefully, so that ethnic identity (or other imperative identities, such as gender or age) become more or less irrelevant.

In certain societies, and in certain historical situations, it may never the less be nearly impossible to escape from ethnic identification. It comes from outside, from the state, or from the more powerful groups which set the agenda in society. Somali refugees in western Europe, a strongly stigmatised group of immigrants, can hardly avoid being regarded as primarily Somalis (unless powerful civil rights groups work patiently and cleverly for a change in policy and mentality). To migrants from other European countries, who are not visibly different nor victims of strongly pejorative views, it may be easier to undercommunicate one's ethnic identity. Generally, in societies where politics are strongly ethnicised, like Fiji or Mauritius, ethnic identity may be the first thing one notices when meeting a new person. In this kind of situation, ethnic identity is more imperative than situational or rather, the possibilities for situational selection are narrower than elsewhere. (Note that ethnicity does not necessarily have anything to do with appearance; Croats, Serbs and Bosnians look the same.)

The question concerning coercion and choice – the imperative and the situational – is a complex one. The Scandinavian school in ethnicity research has been criticised for emphasising individual choice too much, thereby neglecting external pressures and oppression in the study of identification. This accusation is partly relevant, but it must be added that the concept of *ethnic stigma* was introduced by Eidheim, and that many anthropologists who have worked in a situationalist framework have also been active in the international indigenous people's movement, which fights structural violence.

How much of the identity package of any individual is chosen, and how much is enforced? It is common to think that some group memberships, like kinship, ethnic identity, mother tongue and gender, are imperative (enforced), while others are chosen relatively freely. However, there are some tricky transitions, complexities and intermediate zones here, which make it difficult to draw a clear boundary. If the *content* of, say, gender identity is subject to negotiation, then how enforced is one's gender (or sex)? 'Female rebellions' are, perhaps, chiefly associated with modern feminism, but they are far from unknown in traditional societies as well. In contemporary western European societies, a powerful popular opposition towards arranged marriages has emerged over the last few years; a custom practised among some immigrants (and, naturally, in their countries of origin). The argument against arranged marriage is that marriage is supposed to be based on free choice and true love. But how freely chosen are the marriages of the majority in western societies? All research indicates that people marry within their social class and their cultural milieu, and that powerful informal norms regulate the relationship between the spouses.

A difference is that arranged marriages involve entire kin groups woven together through ties of reciprocity, while 'love' or freely chosen marriages only involve two individuals. Another important difference is that the price of refusing an arranged marriage can be much higher than the price for choosing to live alone in a context where freely chosen marriages are the norm. But even in many modern, western societies, the social cost of living alone can be considerable. As so often in anthropology, we must look for relationships based on trust and reciprocity to gauge the centrality of a particular practice in someone's life.

Imperative identities are rarely completely imperative – it is always possible to twist or manipulate their content – and chosen identities are not entirely chosen either. Yet it may be relevant to distinguish them from each other. In general, the imperative element is stronger in traditional societies than in modern ones. Most actually existing societies are mixed, complex sociocultural forms, where there are ongoing conflicts, compromises and competitions between what we may call different criteria of identification. In most places where people live – from Indonesian *kampungs* to Colombian cities, from South African townships to Alaskan hamlets – tugs-of-war are being staged between values presented as traditional and values which emphasise choice and individual freedom. The context is always local and thereby unique, and both the power of tradition and the actual freedom of choice varies dramatically from Borneo to Minnesota. Yet it can be important to insist stubbornly, and to show, that these tensions between the security of tradition and the freedom of modernity have a universal aspect.

DEGREES OF IDENTIFICATION

Above, I raised the question of how it can be that certain identities become so much more important than others. Why is ethnic identity so important in Fiji, when religious identity is more important in Algeria and class identity may be the most important social identification in many parts of Britain; why is national identification so strong in Scotland and Estonia when it is so weak in England and Italy; and how can we begin to account for variations in identification within a single society? It is impossible to give a full answer to these interlinked questions here. Besides, it is often more important to be in the vicinity of the question than believing that one has found the answer. I shall never the less suggest some analytical strategies that make it possible to raise the question(s) in an accurate and, hopefully, fruitful way.

The internal cohesion of a group depends on the degree of external pressure. This principle, formulated early in the twentieth century by the German sociologist Georg Simmel, is sometimes spoken of as 'Simmel's rule'. This simple principle is very useful and often relevant in analysis. First, it may help us to understand why group identity can be strong or weak. In societies with considerable discrepancies between the social strata, such as the classical western class society or the Indian caste society, group identifications along the lines of class or caste will presumably be strong, especially to those who perceive the system as oppressive. If one is born into an ethnic group which has for centuries been kept down by stronger majorities (such as gypsies), it is likely that one will have a clearly delineated ethnic identity. In fact, Simmel's rule may shed light on the fact that Muslim identity has become so powerful globally during the last decades, why the inhabitants of small countries like Catalonia and Estonia by and large have a much stronger national identity than larger countries like Germany and Spain, why gender identity is more often associated with women than with men, and likewise why 'race' somehow seems to concern blacks more than whites. It is because it is the members of these groups who perceive the pressure from outside most strongly. The struggle to survive as an identifiable (and dominant) social entity has hardly been a problem to the English since the Norman invasion, and this is part of the reason that the Welsh and Irish have a far more visible and outspoken ethnic or national identity than their more powerful neighbour. A minority is reminded of its minority status every day, unlike a majority. A Turk in Turkey rarely needs to reflect on his Turkishness; take him to Denmark, and he is confronted with the fact that he is Turkish several times a day. Regarding Islam, it is worth noticing that religious identification – as a social, emblematic form of identity – increased among Muslims after the formation of Israel, and it also seems to be intensified by increased western military activities in Muslim areas.

Second, Simmel's rule does not merely offer a vantage-point for studying the relative strength of group identification; it also invites studies of *the kind of group* that is formed. The character of the group depends on where the pressure is perceived as coming from. There are often rival views within any group in this regard. A classic predicament in the European labour movement is the contrast between class identity and national identity. Should, for instance, German workers have supported the German war preparations in 1914, or should they rather have denounced a war which forced German workers to shoot at their French comrades? Where was the pressure perceived as being the strongest, from the bourgeoisie or from enemy nations? In the remarkable novel *The*

Wall of the Plague, the South African author André Brink describes the encounter between a black freedom fighter and a white feminist, and shows how the struggle between two liberation causes is played out; the white feminist admires the political vision and sense of justice displayed by the anti-apartheid activist, but positively hates his view of women.

The principle of external pressure and internal cohesion may shed light on segmentary forms of organisation. Evans-Pritchard's segmentary model of Nuer politics has been referred to earlier: when the pressure comes from my brother (we argue about our paternal inheritance), it is him against me; when the pressure comes from our cousins (they claim cows we think belong to us), it is my brother and me against them, and so on. Following the outbreak of civil war in Sudan in the early 1980s, between the Muslim North and the non-Muslim South, not only was the entire Nuer people politically united, but they also cooperated uneasily with other southern Sudanese peoples, including their arch-enemies, the Dinka. The pressure was now perceived to exist at such a systemic level that the group kept together was far larger than any earlier political alliance in the region. Simmel's rule also makes it tempting to predict that the alliance will break up the moment the struggle against the 'Arabs' ends.

External pressure does not decide the internal cohesion of a group alone. There must also be something about the internal composition of a group which creates loyalty and commitment. Otherwise, the external pressure will only lead to dissolution and internal conflicts. For a group to function, it must have something to offer to its members, and it must place legitimate demands on them. This 'something' does not have to be political or economic resources; it may also be intangibles deemed necessary for a meaningful, self-respecting existence. But there must be something which creates a willingness to sacrifice, and a sense of solidarity and loyalty among the members. There must be reciprocity and trust. Some kind of resources must flow within the group, it must have a structure of authority which ensures that the norms are followed, and it must justify itself ideologically; it must legitimate its existence. Ethnic leaders appeal to notions about shared origins and blood ties. Religious groups promise eternal salvation and threaten eternal damnation. Other groups may promise honour, wealth, jobs or influence, or they may simply offer security and stability. In stable, traditional societies, these mechanisms were rarely challenged. It is in situations of change, where old values are confronted with new ones, and where a multitude of opportunities becomes visible to the individual, that such processes are most easily seen.

The degree of belonging in a group depends on what it has to offer, both in terms of resources and in terms of sanctions. An extremely tightly integrated group offers practically everything to its members; a place of residence, political influence, a profession or its equivalent, a useful network of trustworthy contacts, a spouse and an overarching religious meaning to life. The price to pay if one opts to break out of such a group is, naturally, high; one risks losing everything, moving back to square one in one's life. An extremely loosely integrated group, on the other hand, may offer nothing but an annual party to its members; the rest of the year, the group members must draw on their other networks of commitment and group memberships. This distinction reminds us of the fact that ethnic identity among Swedish-Americans in the Midwest is something quite different from ethnic identity among Jews in Tunisia.

ANOMALIES

Let us not forget that there are people who do not fit in. Until recently, they have received scant attention from anthropologists. This may be explained by the subject's double heritage; the Boas school's emphasis on the patterned, regular nature of cultural forms, and the British persistence in looking at factors contributing to the integration of societies. The truth is, of course, that neither cultures nor societies hang perfectly together. There are both centripetal (integrative) and centrifugal (divisive) forces at work in any society, from the smallest to the largest and most complex.

Since identification hinges on contrast, most social identities are of the either-or kind. One is either man or woman, either Mexican or Guatemalan, either black or white, Christian or Hindu. That is to say, in theory and according to ideologies of identity politics, that is how it is, or at least ought to be. The real world is much less well ordered.

The population in Trinidad consists of two large ethnic categories (apart from a number of smaller ones), namely Afro-Trinidadians and Indo-Trinidadians. Those of African origin are Christian (Catholic or Anglican) and are associated with certain cultural values and practices such as the calypso and carnival. The Trinidadians of Indian origin are largely Hindu (but considerable numbers are also Muslim or Christian), and are associated with other cultural values and publicly visible practices such as Indian films and dance. Most Trinidadians fit into one of these large categories, but when one looks closely, few individuals are 'typical' representatives of their group. Among Africans, there are important variations concerning class and colour (which is socially significant in the Caribbean), and among Indians there are perhaps even greater variations following the lines of town/countryside, religion and values associated with individualism. The relative importance of ethnic membership to an individual in 'multi-ethnic Trinidad' varies from hardly anything to nearly everything.

In addition, several interesting, intermediate categories exist. The largest consists of the people known locally as *douglas*. The term comes from bhojpuri (the Hindi-related language spoken by most of the Indian immigrants to Trinidad in the nineteenth century), which means 'bastard'. *Douglas* are 'mixtures'. They have both African and Indian ancestors; usually, they have one parent of each kind. A calypso from 1960, written and performed by an artist who simply used '*Dougla*' as his sobriquet, made explicit the frustration so many Trinidadians felt for not belonging to a clear-cut group or category. The lyrics of the song began with an imagined scenario where the authorities decided that Trinidad was a failed experiment, and that all inhabitants should be sent 'home' to where their ancestors came from. Some would be sent to Africa, some to India, but, as the song went '... what about me? They would have to split me in two'. A *dougla*, the singer goes on to relate, has no place to find protection if there is ethnic fighting, no parties to vote for, no football team to root for, no networks higher up in the hierarchies of society. The *dougla* was a non-person, an ethnic anomaly, the pangolin of ethnic classification.

All identity systems have their *douglas*, functioning partly like the third element in Lévi-Strauss's binary schemes. Ethnic anomalies are those who are both-and and neither-nor. They are neither black nor white, neither Russian nor Chechnyan, or they

are both Christian and Palestinian (like the late Edward Said),
both Pakistani and English. Many years after the performance
of the aforementioned calypso, Trinidadian intellectuals spoke
metaphorically about the 'douglarisation of Trinidadian society'.
They meant that there was by now such a bewildering array of
cultural and social mixtures in Trinidad, that it would soon no
longer make sense to speak of a purely Afro or Indo way of life.

Anthropologists have explored comparable phenomena in many
other societies, using concepts like hybridisation, creolisation or
syncretism to describe them. Such processes of mixing create new
cultural forms, help the ambiguous grey zones proliferate, and
make it increasingly difficult to know where to draw the boundary
between this group and that. On the one hand, it is clear the
hybridisation has deeply challenged the formerly unquestioned
emphasis on boundaries and group cohesion as constitutive for
group cohesion. The ambiguous zones and the fuzzy frontier areas
replace sharp boundaries in many cases. On the other hand, it
is equally clear that boundaries are being re-created and often
strengthened as a reaction to the tendencies towards their erasure
and relativisation. In Mauritius, another multi-ethnic society with
strong tendencies towards cultural mixing, the Catholic bishop
expressed it thus; 'Let the colours be clear and distinct for the
rainbow to remain beautiful'.

Decades of intensive studies of inter-ethnic processes have
shown that there is no reason *a priori* to assume that cultural
exchanges lead to the dissolution of identity boundaries. In fact,
it is often the case that the more similar people become, the more
concerned they are to appear different from each other. And, one
might add, the more different they try to be, the more similar
they become! For there exist some standardised ways of expressing
uniqueness and difference, which are recognised and globally
accepted, and which make different groups comparable. In the
process of rendering oneself comparable, one risks losing some
of the traits that, perhaps, made one distinctive in the first place.
Clothes, food, folk music and folk history are elements which
recur in identity politics almost everywhere. The grammar drawn
upon to express differences is becoming globally standardised.

* * *

With this paradox we shall end, although considerable parts of the vast discipline of anthropology have not even been mentioned. My ambitions in this book have been modest. I have endeavoured to give an overview, a handful of concepts from classic and current research and – perhaps most importantly – to convey that anthropology is a way of thinking. As such it is concerned with how humans make sense of their world, emphasising the power of symbols and narratives; and how social life can be regular, predictable and a source of security, emphasising the importance of trust and reciprocity. There are other anthropologies – anthropologies of medicine, of nationalism and the state, of religion and of development, to mention but a few – but they, too, belong to the same broad tradition of thinking presented here.

Personally, I am convinced that the kind of cross-cultural, comparative thought and cultural self-reflection that anthropology offers, is of fundamental importance in a shrinking world where insider knowledge of the lives of others and a proper understanding of the experiences and ideas of others is in short supply, both among political powerholders and elsewhere. In addition, there is no doubt that anthropology is a subject which has the potential to change the lives of those who choose to enter it.

FURTHER READING

Barth, Fredrik, ed. (1969) *Ethnic Groups and Boundaries: The Social Organization of Culture Difference.* Oslo: Universitetsforlaget.
Eriksen, Thomas Hylland (2002) *Ethnicity and Nationalism: Anthropological Perspectives*, 2nd edition. London: Pluto.

Bibliography

Anderson, Benedict (1983) *Imagined Communities. An Inquiry into the Origins and Spread of Nationalism.* London: Verso.

Archetti, Eduardo (1984) Om maktens ideologi – en krysskulturell analyse. (On the ideology of power – a cross-cultural analysis). In Arne Martin Klausen, ed. *Den norske væremåten* (The Norwegian way of being). Oslo: Cappelen.

Arens, William (1978) *The Man-eating Myth. Anthropology and Anthropophagy.* Oxford: Oxford University Press.

Barley, Nigel (1986 [1983]) *The Innocent Anthropologist: Notes From a Mud Hut.* Harmondsworth: Penguin.

Barnes, John (1962) African Models in New Guinea Highlands. *Man*, vol. 5: 5–9.

Barth, Fredrik (1966) *Models of Social Organization.* London: Royal Anthropological Institute, Occasional Papers, no. 23.

—— ed. (1969) *Ethnic Groups and Boundaries. The Social Organization of Culture Difference.* Oslo: Scandinavian University Press.

Bateson, Gregory (1979) *Mind and Nature.* Glasgow: Fontana.

Benedict, Ruth (1934) *Patterns of Culture. Patterns of Culture.* Boston, MA: Houghton Mifflin.

Berreman, Gerald (1962) *Behind Many Masks: Ethnography and Impression Management in a Himalayan Village.* The Society for Applied Anthropology: Monograph no. 4.

Bohannan, Laura (1952) A Genealogical Charter. *Africa*, vol. 22: 301–15.

Bohannan, Paul (1959) The Impact of Money on an African Subsistence Economy. *Journal of Economic History*, vol. 19: 491–503.

Bourdieu, Pierre (1977) *Outline of a Theory of Practice*, trans. Richard Nice. Cambridge: Cambridge University Press.

—— 1990 [1980] *The Logic of Practice*, trans. Richard Nice. Cambridge: Polity.

Brink, Andre (1985) *The Wall of the Plague.* London: Flamingo.

Daly, Martin and Margo Wilson (1988) *Homicide.* New York: de Gruyter.

Darwin, Charles (1979 [1872]) *The Expression of Emotions in Man and Animals.* London: Friedman.

Diamond, Jared (1992) *The Third Chimpanzee: The Evolution and Future of the Human Animal.* New York: HarperCollins.

Douglas, Mary (1966) *Purity and Danger.* London: Routledge and Kegan Paul.

Durkheim, Emile and Marcel Mauss (1963 [1903]) *Primitive Classification*, trans. Rodney Needham. London: Cohen and West.

Døving, Runar (2001) Kaffe – enklere enn vann. En analyse av ytelse i Torsvik. (Coffee – simpler than water. An analysis of prestations in Torsvik) *Norsk antropologisk tidsskrift*, vol. 12, no. 4.

Eidheim, Harald (1971) *Aspects of the Lappish Minority Situation.* Oslo: Universitetsforlaget.

Eriksen, Thomas Hylland, ed. (2003) *Globalisation – Studies in Anthropology.* London: Pluto.

Evans-Pritchard, E.E. (1983 [1937]) *Witchcraft, Magic and Oracles among the Azande.* Oxford: Oxford University Press.

Evans-Pritchard, E.E. (1956) *Nuer Religion.* Oxford: Clarendon.

Firth, Raymond (1951) *Elements of Social Organization.* London: Watts.

Fortes, Meyer and E.E. Evans-Pritchard, eds. (1940) *African Political Systems.* Oxford: Oxford University Press.

Frazer, James (1890) *The Golden Bough: A Study in Magic and Religion.* London: Macmillan. (Published in many later editions.)

Geertz, Clifford (1973) *The Interpretation of Cultures.* New York: Basic Books.

Giddens, Anthony (1984) *The Constitution of Society.* Cambridge: Polity.

Gluckman, Max (1982 [1956]) *Custom and Politics in Africa.* Oxford: Blackwell.

Godelier, Maurice (1999) *The Enigma of the Gift.* Nora Scott. Cambridge: Polity.

Hannerz, Ulf (1992) *Cultural Complexity.* New York: Columbia University Press.

—— (1996) *Transnational Connections.* London: Routledge.

Harris, Marvin (1965) The Myth of the Sacred Cow. In Anthony Leeds and Andrew P. Vayda, eds. *Man, Culture, and Animals.* Washington: American Association for the Advancement of Science.

—— (1998) *Theories of Culture in Postmodern Times.* Walnut Creek: AltaMira Press.

Headland, Thomas, Kenneth L. Pike and Marvin Harris, eds. (1990) *Emics and Etics: The Insider–Outsider Debate.* London: Sage.

Holy, Ladislav (1996) *Anthropological Perspectives on Kinship.* London: Pluto.

Howell, Signe and Roy Willis, eds. (1989) *Societies at Peace: Anthropological Perspectives.* London: Routledge.

Hviding, Edvard (1996) *Guardians of Marovo Lagoon: Practice, Place and Politics in Maritime Melanesia.* Honolulu: University of Hawaii Press.

Ingold, Tim (1994) Introduction to Social Life. In Tim Ingold, ed. *Companion Encyclopedia of Anthropology: Humanity, Culture and Social Life,* pp. 735–37. London: Routledge.

Jones, Steve (1997) *In the Blood: God, Genes and Destiny.* London: Flamingo.

Kalland, Arne (1993) Whale politics and green legitimacy: A critique of the anti-whaling campaign. *Anthropology Today,* vol. 9, no. 6.

Kluckhohn, Clyde (1944) *Navaho Witchcraft.* Cambridge, Mass.: The Peabody Museum.

—— and Alfred Kroeber (1952) *Culture: A Critical Review of Concepts and Definitions.* Cambridge, MA: Harvard University Press.

Kuper, Adam (1999) *Culture. The Anthropologist's Account.* Cambridge, MA: Harvard University Press.

Leach, Edmund R. (1954) *Political Systems of Highland Burma.* London: Athlone.

Lévi-Strauss, Claude (1969 [1949]) *The Elementary Structures of Kinship,* trans. Rodney Needham. London: Tavistock.

Lévi-Strauss, Claude (1966 [1962]) *The Savage Mind.* Chicago: University of Chicago Press.

Lien, Marianne (1992) Nytte, normer og forståelse. (Utility, norms and understanding) *Norsk Antropologisk Tidsskrift*, vol. 3, no. 1.

Lienhardt, Godfrey (1985) From Study to Field, and Back. *Times Literary Supplement*, 7 June.

Malinowski, Bronislaw (1984 [1922]). *Argonauts of the Western Pacific*. Prospect Heights: Waveland.

Mauss, Marcel (1954 [1925]) *The Gift*, trans. Ian Cunnison. London: Routledge and Kegan Paul.

—— (1979) *Sociology and Anthropology*. London: Routledge.

Mead, Margaret (1949 [1928]) *Coming of Age in Samoa*. New York: Mentor.

Mead, Margaret (1973 [1930]) *Growing up in New Guinea*. Harmondsworth: Penguin.

Miller, Daniel (1998) *A Theory of Shopping*. Cambridge: Polity.

Mills, C. Wright (1979 [1959]) *The Sociological Imagination*. Harmondsworth: Penguin.

Nadel, S. F. (1952) Witchcraft in Four African Societies: An Essay in Comparison. *American Anthropologist*, vol. 54: 18–29.

Polanyi, Karl (1944) *The Great Transformation: The Political and Economic Origins of Our Time*. Beacon Hill: Beacon Press.

Radcliffe-Brown, A. R. (1952 [1924]) The mother's brother in South Africa. In Radcliffe-Brown: *Structure and Function in Primitive Society*. London: Cohen and West.

Reddy, G. Prakash (1992) *'Sådan er danskerne': en indisk antropologs perspektiv på det danske samfund*. ('Such are the Danes': An Indian anthropologist's perspective on Danish society). Mørke: Grevas.

Ridley, Matt (1996) *The Origins of Virtue*. London: Viking.

Sahlins, Marshall D. (1972) *Stone Age Economics*. Chicago: Aldine.

—— (1977) *The Use and Abuse of Biology*. Chicago: University of Chicago Press.

—— (1994) Goodbye to Tristes Tropes: Ethnography in the Context of Modern World History. In Robert Borofsky, ed. *Assessing Cultural Anthropology*, pp. 377–94. New York: McGraw-Hill.

Strathern, Marilyn (1992) *After Nature. English Kinship in the Late Twentieth Century*. Cambridge: Cambridge University Press.

Tylor, E. B. (1958 [1871]) *Primitive Culture*. Abridged edition. New York: Harper.

Weiner, Annette (1976) *Women of Value, Men of Renown: New Perspectives in Trobriand Exchange*. Austin: University of Texas Press.

—— (1992) *Inalienable Possessions. The Paradox of Keeping-while-giving*. Berkeley: University of California Press.

Wilson, Edward O. (1975) *Sociobiology: The New Synthesis*. Cambridge, MA: Harvard University Press.

Winch, Peter (1958) *The Idea of a Social Science and its Relation to Philosophy*. London: Routledge.

Worsley, Peter (1997) *Knowledges: What Different Peoples Make of the World*. London: Profile.

Index

Compiled by Sue Carlton